Drama 3–5

A practical guide
to teaching drama to
children in the Early
Years Foundation Stage

Second edition

Debbie Chalmers

Routledge
Taylor & Francis Group

LONDON AND NEW YORK

Second edition published 2015
by Routledge
2 Park Square, Milton Park, Abingdon, Oxon OX14 4RN

and by Routledge
711 Third Avenue, New York, NY 10017

Routledge is an imprint of the Taylor & Francis Group, an informa business

© 2015 Debbie Chalmers

First edition published by Routledge 2007

British Library Cataloguing in Publication Data
A catalogue record for this book is available from the British Library

Library of Congress Cataloging in Publication Data
Chalmers, Debbie, 1966–.
Drama 3–5: a practical guide to teaching drama to children in the
early years foundation stage/Debbie Chalmers. – Second edition.
pages cm
Includes index.
1. Drama – Study and teaching (Elementary) I. Title.
II. Title: Drama three to five.
PN1701.C43 2015
372.66′044 – dc23
2014012608

ISBN: 978-1-138-80535-4 (hbk)
ISBN: 978-1-138-80536-1 (pbk)
ISBN: 978-1-315-75241-9 (ebk)

Typeset in Perpetua and Bell Gothic
by Florence Production Ltd, Stoodleigh, Devon, UK

Printed and bound in the United States of America by Publishers Graphics,
LLC on sustainably sourced paper.

Drama 3–5

Would you like to offer constructive, creative and exciting new dramatic learning experiences to the children in your setting?

The importance of using drama to promote active and creative learning in the early years is widely recognised, and this fully updated second edition of *Drama 3–5* will guide and inspire practitioners in all settings, allowing them to lead drama with confidence and enthusiasm. Young children participating in well planned drama activities learn to express themselves clearly and develop strong social skills, more self-confidence and a greater understanding of co-operation and teamwork.

Drama 3–5 contains a wide range of accessible activities and sample session plans drawn from the author's many years of extensive experience, which have all been fully and successfully tried and tested with children from 3–5 years. The book also explains the theory and value of all of the activities, as well as possible extensions and the ways in which they contribute to the learning objectives and goals of the Early Years Foundation Stage, allowing practitioners to encourage and assess children's progress. Key chapters include:

- Building confidence
- Encouraging social interaction
- Mime and expression
- Speech and language
- Co-operation and teamwork
- Performance skills.

This book offers the tools and understanding needed for confident dramatic play and learning, making it an ideal companion to support every practitioner who wants to explore, develop and enjoy drama and have fun with their children.

Debbie Chalmers is an early years practitioner, a drama teacher and consultant, and a freelance early years and primary education writer.

Essential Guides for Early Years Practitioners

Contents

Introduction

Opportunities for drama and imaginative role play have never been more vital to the learning and development of children up to the age of five. This may be especially true in England and Wales since the Department for Education introduced the Statutory Framework for the Early Years Foundation Stage (EYFS – May 2008; reformed September 2012), but its themes, principles and practice, characteristics of effective learning and areas of development are relevant to the experiences of all young children.

THEMES, PRINCIPLES AND PRACTICE

Practitioners who recognise every child as a unique child will encourage them to create their own characters and scenarios and to try out different roles and experiences, in order to develop greater confidence and a positive sense of their own identity, while valuing and respecting others. Dramatic and imaginative play can be stimulating and responsive, adapting to each child's feelings and interests and encouraging both adult-led and child-initiated ideas, while fostering independence and positive relationships. Throughout the early years, enabling environments will offer relevant and exciting resources, in which children may explore and learn by expressing themselves and designing their own pretend games, as well as enjoying opportunities to work as a group and share music, movement, singing, dance, rhythm, speech activities and drama at all levels.

CHARACTERISTICS OF EFFECTIVE LEARNING

Children demonstrate engagement when they explore and find out. They may use drama to satisfy their curiosity; use their senses; develop interests; pretend that objects are other things; or take on roles and act out experiences, alone and with others. Children's motivation increases when they learn actively, maintaining energy, focus, concentration and persistence. Drama can be challenging, detailed and continuously evolving to allow children to remain stimulated, to solve their own problems and to meet their own challenges. Learning to create and to think critically encourages children to predict and test ideas, to notice links and sequences and to understand cause and effect. Drama activities can allow children to make choices, to try out new ways of doing things, to adapt and change their strategies and to discover a sense of pride and satisfaction in their own achievements, through working with or performing to others.

AREAS OF LEARNING AND DEVELOPMENT

Through sharing drama activities, children can develop skills linked to every area of learning and development within the EYFS. These skills may be most obvious within the prime areas of Physical Development and Communication and Language and in the specific area of Expressive Arts and Design, but learning within the specific areas of Literacy, Mathematics and Understanding the World can also be easily stimulated through the choice of appropriate songs and stories and imaginative use of space.

However, it is in the prime area of Personal, Social and Emotional Development that many young children gain the most, as they grow in confidence and self-esteem and learn to work together with others. Even the shyest children or those with very little social experience will enjoy either singing, dancing, making expressions or joining in with stories within a group, when they do not feel that anyone is looking to judge or compare. Children learn best when they are enjoying themselves.

The inclusion of group drama sessions within the EYFS enriches the curriculum for all children, as practitioners now recognise the value and importance of dramatic and imaginative role play. However, not all practitioners will feel confident to lead in this area and will need to actively seek information, guidance and support, as well as inspiring ideas for activities and suggestions for appropriate materials and resources they might use.

The suggestions and activities in this book can be used by all childcare and education professionals who wish to lead drama sessions with children aged three to five. They are equally suitable for use in a day nursery, pre-school, children's centre or childminding setting, or in a nursery or reception class in a state or independent school.

Each activity may be adapted to match the needs of the children taking part. Sessions may be planned to specifically target the age group contained within one class or to be flexible enough to accommodate a group of children of mixed ages. It will also be possible to make links between dramatic activities and other areas of learning and to make available opportunities for individual imaginative and role play for those children who choose to extend their drama experiences.

Early years practitioners should always seek to provide flexible and open-ended resources and enough time and space to use them, along with the warm and supportive relationships, confident leadership and stimulating and inspiring ideas that will encourage their children to learn and have fun through sharing drama.

Chapter 1

A good beginning

Young children are naturally dramatic. They learn about the world and make sense of their experiences through acting out scenes in the role play area or with small world figures, where they may choose and develop characters, try them out, enjoy them and then discard them in favour of the next game. Some children naturally play in this way from a very young age, often because they have been encouraged to do so at home, while others learn to do it by copying and joining in with their peers. Some children will need more help and support as they may find this type of play more challenging and do not choose it spontaneously.

Opportunities for drama with the right equipment, a well-planned programme, some good ideas, confidence, flexibility and lots of enthusiasm make a vital contribution to the development of all children.

BEFORE EACH SESSION

Allow time to set up your equipment and prepare your space. Ensure that the room you are using is cleared of all furniture and toys that could present a safety risk or a distraction factor. Children will only appreciate drama as an activity in its own right if they are encouraged to move around and concentrate on stories and songs in a large, clear space. There should be no danger of them bumping into tables and chairs or losing concentration because they are looking longingly at rows of inviting toys on shelves or the floor!

When arranging private classes, it is a good idea to make a selection of children's books available before sessions begin, so that clients are prepared to arrive in good time, knowing that they will have something to do with their child and will not feel embarrassed to stand around waiting or struggle to control their child who sees a large empty space and wants to run around. A calm moment spent reading a story or looking at a book can put children into a focused frame of mind from which they will be receptive to a drama session, while running around in a hall is likely to over excite or tire them and lead to accidents and upsets before the session begins.

Providing photograph albums from previous terms, showing photographs of (unnamed) children taken in classes, performances and parties with parents' permission, can be a wonderful talking point between clients and children. Older members of the class grow in self-esteem by seeing themselves in your 'special book' and can be asked to find themselves and their friends and explain what was going on in the pictures to newer members, whose ambition then becomes to have their photograph in your book too!

However, always remember to ask for permission before taking photographs of children and provide a simple way for parents to refuse if they need to. They could talk privately to you or to any staff member, or write their name on a list that you have provided. In this way, parents will not feel embarrassed to withhold their permission and can feel confident that they will not be asked to explain their reasons before other parents.

It is possible to sensitively exclude young children from photographs without their knowledge if necessary, to avoid them becoming upset or feeling unwanted. For example, you could point the camera in their direction too, but never press the button; take pictures when they are at the far side of a group and just outside the frame; take pictures but then erase them from a digital camera; or give all of the pictures to the child's parent.

Looking at photographs can be an excellent opportunity for you to chat informally with children in a friendly way. You may find out that the shy child who is not yet able to answer any questions within the group actually has extremely well-developed language skills and mature understanding, or that the child who appeared to be paying little attention last week remembers every song and character mentioned.

MANAGING TIME

It is important to start on time, being flexible by two or three minutes. If a child is just taking off their coat or using the toilet, it is courteous to wait for them to join the group. If a client has requested your advice or indicated their need to give you some information about their child, it is

FIGURE 1.1 Families enjoy sharing books and photographs before a session begins

not appropriate to end the conversation by looking at the clock, unless you feel that more than a minute or two will be required and you can offer to talk after the session instead.

If clients see that you never start on time because you wait for those who are regularly late, they will all begin to arrive later and later and sessions will run into difficulties. However, it is important to let clients know that if they are sometimes late, they are still able to join in at whatever point you have reached and to make the child feel that they are always welcome.

Since parents are paying for a whole session, you must ensure they have the time you promised. But, if they have a commitment immediately after the class, such as collecting another child from school, they will find it worrying to attend if you run late and do not finish within five minutes of the time agreed. Clients do not continue with a class in the long term if they find fitting it into their schedule too stressful.

It may be appropriate to mention some very special news to the group before beginning – such as a child's birthday on that very day or a new baby sibling born since the last time you saw a child – but discourage children from expecting to think up a tale about a very minor event with which to regale the entire group every week, as this wastes too much precious learning time and causes fidgeting and loss of focus at the wrong time.

If you make it clear to children that you would like to talk to them and hear what they have to say after the drama session, take care to remember and listen as promised; they will usually be happy to wait. This is an excellent opportunity for children to learn how and when to make appropriate conversation and to practise temporary postponement of gratification.

INCLUDING EVERYBODY

When children come together to begin a drama session, they need to feel that they are all equally important and valued within the group and that others are pleased they have come. Confident, talkative children will want their teacher to listen to their latest news or answer their questions, while quieter children may hope that you will notice their toy or new T-shirt or hairstyle. Others may not wish to be the centre of attention or may even be wearing a very attractive garment that they happen to dislike. The aim here is to comment only on the things that children would like you to mention – this gets easier with practice, but nobody gets it right every time!

Through your day to day conversations with parents, carers and colleagues, you will know when a child is feeling particularly tired or fragile, excited or very energetic, coping with an upheaval or trauma or disappointed that their best friend is absent. Background information enables you to make allowances for certain behaviours, accept that a child is temporarily making slower progress, or offer extra support or challenges and stimulation to ensure that children can derive maximum benefit from each session.

Check that the floor is safe and clean enough to work on. It would be unusual to find a nursery with an unsafe floor surface, but some shared settings may have the use of a hall with a wooden floor. Children should always wear shoes if there is any danger of splinters and never just slippery socks or tights to dance on a polished floor. Remember that you may want to include activities such as sliding like a caterpillar, pretending to ice skate, crawling on hands and knees like an animal or rolling in imaginary mud or leaves.

Carpet is not the best floor surface for drama activities, as it does not allow satisfying sounds when stamping and jumping and can harbour dust that could affect allergic children. However, it is safe and can be used if there is no alternative. Vacuum the carpeted area before the children's arrival to ensure cleanliness, safety and to allow dust time to settle. If you are using a hard floor surface, ensure that it will not be too cold or too warm for children to stand, sit and lie on and remind children to take especial care not to fall and bump their heads.

Pre-schools, crèches or children's centres may find it appropriate for children to participate in drama activities in smaller groups and choose to use a room that is separate from the main play areas, if they have one. They may even find that the best large and non-distracting space available to them is an entrance hall or lobby area. Childminders will need to clear or adapt spaces within their homes to allow a group of children to act, dance and move around safely. For some rooms, it might be a good idea to purchase a rug or piece of carpet, vinyl or plastic that may be unrolled for each drama session. Schools and settings within community centres may have access to large PE mats, which are excellent as they will not slip and can break the impact of a fall.

Action songs don't need a great deal of space, but provide healthy exercise and opportunities to learn and practise new skills. Speech, singing, rhythm activities and using percussion instruments are easily explored while children move between the formations of a circle, line or group and individual spaces. Standing up or sitting down changes the situation and the focus enough to recapture a young child's interest. Stories, rhymes or poems may be acted out within a very small area and working close to each other can add to the atmosphere of concentration and fun. Drama can be shared successfully within a smaller space and, with support, children quickly learn to adjust their speed and direction to negotiate a safe pathway around each other. This is a learning objective within the prime area of Physical Development (Moving and handling).

At other times, children may be encouraged to experiment further with different ways of moving within a large space and to participate in racing, chasing and dancing games outside, in the garden or at the park. Clean grass is a safe surface for children to use and mats may be placed under and beside equipment where safety surfaces have not been installed. Drama activities such as imaginative games and role play should also take place outside and can involve large resources including wheeled toys, climbing equipment, tents and dens, which encourage children to pretend to be different people, characters or animals and support the creation of scenarios, sequences and stories. These will contribute to the early learning goals within the specific areas of Understanding the World (People and communities) and Expressive Arts and Design (Being imaginative).

MAINTAINING RELATIONSHIPS

As you will need to prepare your drama sessions in advance, ensure that colleagues understand the importance of sticking to agreed times and giving the full length of time promised to each session. Settings offering part-time sessions to their children must follow their timetable and complete activities, as well as allowing enough time for free flow play, before the children are collected. Those offering full daycare will also have a routine of activities, free playtimes, meals and rest periods that they need to adhere to. Agree with colleagues how long each group of children might concentrate and enjoy drama activities, starting with slightly shorter sessions and gradually building up to longer ones if this is their first experience of drama.

The staff team should make time to chat with each other for a few moments at the beginning and end of each session. It is good for children to see that the adults in their setting get on well, respect each other and work together consistently for the good of the group. A friendly relationship will ensure that both you and they feel happy to raise and discuss any areas of potential concern before they become problems. In this way difficulties can be minimised or prevented. Seek advice on identifying areas where extra support may benefit a child by chatting with the appropriate key person. You will be able to offer each other valuable insights into a child's behaviour and abilities, to record and confirm areas of progress and celebrate achievements. This may be particularly helpful for children with special needs.

Some children who are unable to overcome shyness or communicate with others can 'find a voice' and thrive through exploring drama. Others find it a good area for channelling their energies and demonstrating their creative potential, showing concentration and imaginative skills previously undiscovered in other activities.

If you share your lesson plans with your colleagues, they will be more able to support your teaching and also develop possible extension activities for children who have enjoyed the themes they worked on in drama. Offering a few weeks of lesson plans at a time and in advance may facilitate the best co-operative working between you.

Students, apprentices, trainees and voluntary staff should be particularly encouraged to participate in music, singing, movement, dance and drama sessions, as they can quickly lose inhibitions, be inspired to offer ideas and develop greater confidence when working with groups of children in this way. It will be necessary to have realistic expectations of their abilities at first and to take pleasure in their developing skills and confidence along with the children's, but do make it clear from the beginning that all adults

FIGURE 1.2 Encourage the children to start each session with happy, smiling faces

must participate fully and encourage all children to join in and work to the best of their abilities. It is unacceptable for them to talk to each other about unrelated topics, display embarrassment when acting or singing, or to allow children to 'opt out' and sit on their laps to watch! Enthusiasm and co-operation are the most important skills to maintain throughout.

In a nursery, pre-school, children's centre or school setting, children will have arrived and settled in before their drama class begins, so they will all arrive in the room as a group at the agreed time. It is important to greet all children and staff warmly and indicate how pleased you are to see that they are all ready for their drama session.

Suitable opening comments might be:

I'm so pleased to see that you are ready with such happy smiling faces.

I was glad when I remembered it was Tuesday today, because it's our drama day.

Isn't it lovely to have this room all ready for us to use for dancing, acting and singing?

I've brought my special bag of things for us to look at later.

I remembered how good you all were at being cats last week and I was excited to think about which animals we might be today.

Chapter 2

Warming up

You will need to indicate that your session is about to officially begin in an obvious way. This may involve asking for adults' and children's help in clearing a large enough working space by tidying away a previous activity or moving any furniture, toys and equipment that could be distracting or dangerous to small heads or eyes, or letting clients or colleagues know that you have prepared the equipment and the space and they should now bring the children into the room.

Encourage everybody to come together and sit comfortably in a circle, checking that every child can see and be seen by you and the other members of the group. Ensure that all children have enough space and will be able to use their bodies without bumping into each other or feeling cramped. It doesn't matter how big the circle grows – just encourage children to shuffle outwards until they all have room! Take any child who benefits from extra support to sit beside you at first, or ensure they are beside their key person or another appropriate adult, but do this as unobtrusively as possible and encourage the child not to continue to rely on this level of support as their confidence grows. Never allow sitting beside you or another adult to become a status symbol or a source of competition or rivalry between children, or somebody will inevitably become unhappy.

It is important to greet all children, younger siblings and accompanying adults as they walk through the door and indicate that you are pleased to see them all. Suitable greetings might be:

We're so pleased to see you, Eleanor, because you're so good at singing.

Toby was hoping you'd be here today, Thomas, because you were such good friends last week.

I saw your Daddy yesterday, Daisy, and he told me how much you were looking forward to coming to drama today.

I remember how good you are at being a bear, George, and I thought we might do some more work on bears today.

If a child arrives late, help them to integrate immediately with a statement such as:

Come and join us, Alfie! You're just in time for our listening game!

We must have sung so beautifully that Ruben heard us and came quickly to join in!

STARTING A SESSION

To start a session in a happy way and put everybody into a constructive and co-operative mood, you can use an action song. The song chosen may be familiar to the children or completely new, but it needs to be cheerful and invite enthusiastic joining in. This contributes to the specific area of Expressive Arts and Design (Exploring and using media and materials).

If you begin with the same song at each session, even the youngest child will come to associate it with the activities that follow and feel ready to work on drama. Choose a song that you think the adults will also enjoy, as they may need to model the correct level of enthusiasm and participation for some children at first. For this reason, it may be best to avoid the songs that appear most frequently on every children's CD and are the 'standard diet' at nurseries, pre-schools, children's centres and parent and toddlers' groups, at the very beginning of a session. Children need to know these songs, but you should also aim to make your sessions a little more special.

Changing the song you use as your 'opening number' each half term or every six weeks allows a good balance between the safe and familiar and the new challenge. But you should be prepared to be flexible about this. If you know that the children and adults are still enjoying working on a song that was brand new to them only a few weeks ago, stay with it. But, if you sense that children or adults are becoming bored with a song that they all know well, introduce a new one, or alternate between two or three for a while, so that nobody knows exactly which song it will be on a particular day.

Most importantly, ensure that you choose 'opening numbers' you like and feel totally confident to deliver and lead. If you are a confident and accomplished singer, do feel free to display this ability. Others feel inspired to join in with this type of performance and often surprise themselves. If you are aware that your singing ability is more limited, select songs that allow you to lead through speech and actions and let a CD carry the tune.

First impressions are very important. At any session, you may have at least one child and/or adult who has never attended before and they will not benefit very much until they start enjoying themselves and wanting to participate. Remember, it is much easier to achieve a downward spiral than an upward one, so you want everybody to begin 'on a high' and stay there as long as possible before coming down gradually, rather than trying to climb up as a session progresses. Keep more difficult or less exciting work for the middle of a session.

MAKING INTRODUCTIONS

While children are fairly new to you, you may want to move quickly into your first song with little introduction, but, if you know them well, your relationship will often benefit from some 'standing jokes' and 'pretend mistakes'. Speak to the seated circle as a whole group and allow any child to answer you if they wish to. You may want to begin with phrases such as:

Have you all brought your hands today?

Did anybody bring their feet?

Let's give our mouths a wriggle to warm them up!

Then move on to:

How many hands have you brought?

We need these! What are they? (touching your ears)

Is your face ready? Feel it carefully to make sure it's all there!

11

And work up to:

Now everybody needs their three legs . . .

We're going to tap our noses! (while tapping your knees)

We need ten of something in our song – what could we use?

At first, children will enjoy just shouting out 'No!' and correcting you. But, very soon, more confident and experienced children will be keen to tell you that they've got ten arms today or no feet, or that they've forgotten to bring their face! They love to hear you say that they'd better run home and fetch them quickly, or that they should bring the spare one out from their pocket, or to pretend to 'catch' the spare one that you 'throw' to them and they will carefully mime the 'putting on' of the correct body part because they are already deeply involved in the imaginative game.

You need to monitor this joking and pretending carefully to ensure that it only continues for a few moments and that no child becomes worried or irritated by it. But sharing laughs with lots of children and the firm agreement that 'we are all ready now' is the most enthusiastic and co-operative start you can hope for.

You need not always sit in a circle for your opening number. You could jump up when the music starts and perform it standing up or in your own spaces, or vary it from week to week. Including lots of varied movements and sounds will warm up young children's bodies, mouths and voices successfully. They are unlikely to agree to participate in any specialised physical or vocal exercises with any enthusiasm at this age.

Having warmed everybody up with a busy action song, it is a good idea to follow it immediately with a calmer one that may be more well-known but demands finer movements, such as using fingers and thumbs or hands and heads to fit the song words. This song should, ideally, be different at each session, but all of the songs could be repeated after a term or a period of ten to twelve weeks.

Young children particularly like songs and games involving hiding their hands and making them pop out again at the right time, counting on their fingers, clapping, stamping and shaking their heads. They also enjoy trying new things that they would like to learn to do, such as snapping their fingers or clapping behind their backs. As long as you make it clear that this is more difficult and most of them are still learning, they will happily understand that they should just try their best and accept praise for effort

■ **FIGURE 2.1** Get sessions off to an enthusiastic start using lively action songs and finger rhymes

and small advances. This is excellent preparation for later life, when they will be asked to practise and improve some skills that do not come easily to them and they will need to have a positive attitude to everybody being good at certain things and less good at others.

MONITORING FRIENDSHIPS

During a warming up period, you will notice which children are close friends and whether they rely too heavily on doing things together. If you have a child who always copies another, or a pair of children who only speak to each other or constantly giggle together instead of listening to others, you will need to decide the extent to which this may become a problem. On a day that one of the pair is feeling tired, slightly unwell or over-excited, the other will also be adversely affected, or if one is absent from a session, the other may be unwilling to join in constructively.

While recognising and accepting the importance of children's friendships, you need to encourage them to gradually work more independently.

■ **FIGURE 2.2** Recognise the importance of children's friendships, but encourage them to work independently too

Any of us can feel happier in a situation with a familiar person present, but this needs to be seen as a valuable confidence booster that we can 'jump off from', not used as an excuse to lean on someone else or to have an accomplice in being disruptive! In order for children to achieve their full potential and feel proud of what they do, they must learn to think and behave in the way that is right for them – not for their next door neighbour or the person they sit with at school.

You might start by asking the pair of friends if another child could sit between them in the circle or if they could each have a particular child beside them. Being asked to demonstrate a skill to help a younger or newer child may give them both the necessary incentive to separate and apply themselves to the task individually. However, do make sure that the younger or newer class members will appreciate the help and monitor the relationships involving over-enthusiastic children, to avoid any feelings of intimidation. During action songs, role play and the acting out of stories, offer the friends separate parts and places in lines and groups and let them know that they have been specially chosen for those parts because they are suited to their abilities.

If a group of several friends or classmates are 'sticking together', refusing to participate fully or dominating the group too much, their behaviour may need to be dealt with quite firmly. Explaining in honest and reasonable terms why they must work as individuals within the whole class or group usually works with children from the age of 3 or 4. If they are mature enough to understand how to 'wind each other up', they are also mature enough to understand how and why they should stop!

Always give lots of praise to children as soon as they begin to do as you have asked. Publicly applaud their individual achievements during classes and thank them privately for making any attitude or behaviour changes that were discussed and agreed with you. Children appreciate and remember specific statements of praise much more than generalities. Instead of: 'You were good in the class today, Rebecca' or 'Well done, Finlay', aim for comments such as: 'Well done, Max for sitting next to Oscar as well as Sefton in the circle today' or 'I loved the way you chose to tap your knees, Ruth, while you chose to tap your shoulders, Ellen, during the song'.

When twins, triplets or siblings attend sessions together, their particular relationships must be understood and respected, but they should also be encouraged to behave as individuals, in the same way as friends. Older children must not be expected to regularly care for younger siblings to a degree that their own performances and enjoyment are impaired. A younger sibling may not wish to be smothered by an older sibling's attentions and be quite able to cope with activities without help. One twin or triplet may be more dominant or confident than the other(s) and behave in a similar way to an older sibling.

Discussion with each child's parent, carer or key person will enable you to react in a manner appropriate to the child's needs and also consistent with the other adults' wishes and ideals. You will need to take on the support of the younger or less confident children yourself, or ensure that colleagues are doing so, to enable the others to work individually. You should then be able to increase confidence quickly and allow all children to take appropriate places within the group.

The overall aim during the warming up period is to bring the group together, and to encourage each child to acquire the type of attitude and focused concentration that will enable them to derive maximum benefit from each activity and have fun together. You will be working towards all of the early learning goals within the prime area of Personal, Social and Emotional Development (Self-confidence and self-awareness, Managing feelings and behaviour, Making relationships).

Chapter 3

Building confidence

Drama can help enormously in building confidence at any age. Learning to express yourself more clearly and practising speech and movement skills are valuable aids to developing good self-esteem. Role play situations can help with preparing for or recovering from difficult or worrying experiences, enabling you to 'move on' and use new skills to cope more easily in the future. Developing the imagination and flexibility to adapt to situations quickly and do your best to join in or make things work is an empowering life skill best learned as early as possible.

SPEAKING UP

We would all like our children to have confidence when entering new situations, to feel able to make friends and be a useful member of any group. One of the most basic skills to master is a way of introducing yourself and finding out about the other people around you. You will also want to find out quickly what they are like and be aware of the impression you would like them to form of you. In order for children to feel comfortable with the people they interact with, you can teach them how to give their name and listen to what others are called. You can explain that this is good manners, as well as useful and interesting.

While the children are still sitting or standing in a circle, you can offer your hand to each one in turn, shaking it gently, smiling and saying: 'Hello, my name's Debbie.'

More confident and experienced children will take your hand, shake it in return and reply: 'Hello, my name's Lucy.' Others will take your hand and smile and nod and wait. If they are then prompted with: 'And your name is . . .?', they will reply: 'Daniel!'

FIGURE 3.1 Dramatic introductions enable children to build self-confidence and learn to interact with others

At this point, you can say: 'Nice to see you' or 'I'm glad you came' along with the child's name and then move on to the next person in the circle.

Some children may be happy to say their name, but unwilling to take your hand; or be happy to shake hands but unwilling or unable to say their name yet. Some may, at first, be unwilling to respond at all but pleased to be spoken to. Other children may even hide their faces in embarrassment at the first few classes or ask their parent or carer to say their name for them. The important aim is that each child should understand that they are equally important to you and that everybody is interested in who they are and keen to include them in the group.

Children learn by example and most love to copy others. If you repeat this exercise in a gentle and non-threatening way at each session, with some children responding and others watching and listening, almost all will gradually understand and want to join in. This is another opportunity

17

to encourage children to wait their turn to speak, to listen to each other and to give everybody a fair chance to speak. Those who shout out, supply other children's names for them when not asked to or try to disrupt the 'listening circle' may need additional adult explanation and support to understand why this is not the best way to behave. Practitioners or family members may choose to practise this activity with a child between drama sessions, but should avoid putting pressure on a child to 'get it right next time'!

Adults can be surprised when a child who previously didn't understand or absolutely refused to co-operate suddenly feels able to look at the teacher's face and give a mature reply. However, they should celebrate the achievement of this learning objective sensitively, by rewarding the child with praise, but avoiding making too much fuss.

Once children have attended sessions for a year or two, they may decide to develop the activity by thinking up ever longer and fancier names that they would like to have. If a child wearing a striped T-shirt tells you that his name is 'Stripey', or a girl with a motif on her dress announces herself as 'Butterfly', they have understood that a name is a label and, in many situations, can be their own to use as they wish. A boy who tells the circle that his name is 'Mr Cool', or a girl who announces herself under the name of 'Sparkling Fairy Tiger Lily', is demonstrating intelligence, high self-esteem and, of course, a good sense of humour!

Eventually, children may enjoy passing around a microphone to use when giving their special introductory speech. Children's 'echo mikes' can be purchased cheaply from toy shops and are usually large and chunky, bright and colourful and very attractive to budding stage per-formers. Even the adults are usually keen to try them out! They amplify a voice just enough to make a recognisable difference, without being too off-putting to a nervous child, and can be practised safely and easily and then used confidently onstage in performances.

Teach the children to hold the microphones carefully, as they can break or stop working if they are dropped on a hard floor surface. Demonstrate how close to the mouth they should be held for maximum effect and discourage children from bending their heads down over them or touching their mouths with them. Speak to the children clearly, holding a micro-phone to your own mouth and looking up to make eye contact with your audience. They will learn for themselves that the microphones only work if they hold them not too close, but not too far away and if they remember to look up as they speak. Passing a microphone around also helps children

FIGURE 3.2 Taking turns to use a microphone helps children to understand when to speak and when to listen

to understand when to speak and when to listen, how to wait patiently and how to take turns and share.

Throughout a session, there are numerous opportunities to encourage children to speak up, sometimes as a group and sometimes individually, such as when you ask questions after a mime session. After building up a tower of heavy bricks, ask the group:

Who used more than five bricks?

Whose tower is taller than their head?

Whose tower is wobbling?

Did anybody's tower fall down?

Ask each child individually:

What did you build with your bricks, Kitty?

Alexander, what did you use to stick them together?

Accept all answers as valid – sensible ones show that a child understands the project, but funny answers show that the child understands this is the world of imagination and they are in control. An imaginary tower of bricks and cement is great, but an imaginary tower of cardboard boxes and golden syrup is just as much fun! Such discussions can contribute to learning objectives within the specific area of Mathematics (Shape, space and measures).

Choose questions carefully according to the age, experience level and size of the group of children and be prepared to be flexible. While the group is enjoying the game, continue to ask questions and listen to answers. If they begin to fidget or lose concentration, move on to the next activity, ensuring that each child has had at least one opportunity to speak.

PERFORMANCE SKILLS

It is very valuable for children to experience standing and working onstage. Many adults wish they could have had the opportunity to perform in some way after leaving school, or that they could now join an amateur theatre company or take part in a concert or exhibition, but feel too overcome with embarrassment or lack the confidence in their own abilities, so do not do it. If children are used to standing up before others regularly from a very young age and speaking out, singing, dancing or performing, they will be able to use these skills in any situation they encounter later and never have to miss an opportunity they wish they could have taken.

In a school or nursery setting, you may be lucky enough to have a stage or stage blocks that can be easily assembled for use in at least some of your drama sessions. This may also apply to a hired hall for private classes. If not, try to make a special area, which you can call 'our stage', using gym mats, rugs or blankets, a brick surround or lines chalked on the floor. Children can be encouraged to stand in a line or a group onstage and shout out phrases to any adults or baby siblings forming their audience, or to a picture on the back wall. This ensures that they have no fear of speaking out into a room or hall when they know they have something valid to say. If this fear never develops, it will not crop up in later life. Telling children that important and special people stand onstage and that it makes other people want to listen, as well as joining them and showing your own excitement and pleasure to be on a stage, help to develop the attitude you are aiming for. Suitable phrases to say onstage might be:

Hello everybody!

Welcome to our drama class!

Today is Monday!

Today we've been thinking about jungle animals!

Encourage the children to speak and enunciate clearly and project their voices, rather than shouting as loudly as they can until the sounds and words are lost. They will learn most easily through copying, if you demonstrate the difference between shouting and projecting with a clear voice. You could also offer advice such as 'Talk to the wall at the back of the room', or ask colleagues to stand some distance away and wave when they hear clearly, but cover their ears when they hear only shouting.

Praise those who try particularly hard, whether they are achieving an objective for the first time or reliably improving at each session. Ensure that every child knows what is to be said before you begin and is ready to focus and concentrate. Count them in with 'one, two, three' or 'ready and go' and they will already be beginning to learn about timing and working as a member of a team.

As soon as enough children are ready, ask them to speak individually onstage, taking their cue from whoever is next to them in the line. Explain carefully what to say and expect that each child will be listened to by the others. Ask an adult to stand beside a child who calls out or disrupts others' listening, to model and encourage correct responses and discourage others from copying the unwanted behaviour. If a child is unhappy or unable to participate or listen onstage, ask an adult to take the child into the 'audience' to watch the others and rejoin the group for the next activity.

This is another confidence building activity that children can learn gradually, working towards learning objectives within the prime areas of Communication and Language (Listening and attention, Speaking) and Personal, Social and Emotional Development (Self-confidence and self-awareness, Making relationships). It is extremely rewarding to see a young child who cried when taken onstage for the first time, or one with delayed speech who was unable to say anything at early classes, proudly shouting out their name, age and favourite colour to an audience!

Early sessions could involve phrases such as:

My name is Martha and I'm three.

My name is Luke and I live in Cambridge.

21

FIGURE 3.3 It is rewarding to watch each child develop the confidence to stand and speak clearly onstage

Later sessions could move on to:

My name is Megan and I like blue and red.

My name is Hannah and I like pink crocodiles.

Sessions for experienced children could lead to more detail in speech and acting skills:

My name is Pip and if I was in the jungle I would like to be an elephant! *[accompanied by a demonstration of an elephant]*

My name is Sleeping Beauty and my favourite character in my story is the prince who cuts down the trees to come and give me a kiss and wake me up! *[accompanied by a demonstration of a princess sleeping and/or a prince on his horse cutting through a forest]*

Some children will always think up their own idea, while some will copy the most popular idea or that of whoever is next to them. Sometimes children standing separately will have independently thought up the same idea, but others will only gradually understand what to do and find that coping with their position in the line is enough of a new learning experience for the moment. Accept and praise all contributions, but take particular notice of the child who contributes an original idea that is especially imaginative or apt for the situation.

If a child would like to tell you their idea but is not prepared to say it loudly enough for others to hear, come down to their level and accept the contribution in as enthusiastic a manner as all the others, repeating it aloud for the group to share. It is a good idea to clap each child when they finish speaking and encourage your 'audience' to do so too. This helps them to remember why they are speaking out and makes it clear to the next child that it is definitely their turn now.

Ask children to take a bow before they leave the stage. At first, or when time is short, they can all bow together as a group. Individual bows may be taken once children understand how to take cues from each other and are happy to take their turn alone. This is an opportunity for more applause from you and your 'audience'. Some children may ask to curtsey instead and both boys and girls of this age should be permitted to choose.

Some children will answer any question put to the group and challenge any 'deliberate mistake', so long as nobody, especially the teacher, looks at them directly and asks them by name. Others will only speak up when particularly asked, if they are sure that the other children will wait and listen to them.

Some children are much more confident when seated beside their friend or within a group of children they know well. Others prefer to join a private class and find their own place before assessing the potential for friendships. Sometimes a child will be less confident because their key person is absent or they are attending a class with their mother instead of their nanny, or more confident because today granny has come along to watch the class. Some children are naturally quieter or noisier than others most of the time. Each child will gradually decrease their dependence on the support or presence of their parent or carer as their confidence increases. If they receive careful and appropriate encouragement, they will be able to do this at the pace that is right for them.

The overall aim is for all children, whatever their ages, abilities, levels of experience or degrees of special need, to gradually increase their confidence in themselves and their knowledge that they are worthwhile people. Then they may achieve whatever they wish to, in the way that they feel is right for them, without the frustration of feeling that they 'can't do it'. This is an attitude that will help them throughout their lives.

Chapter 4

Encouraging social interaction

Drama is essentially a social activity. When people act, sing, dance or perform, they seldom do so alone, but are usually members of a group or team who work together to create a whole experience. Luckily, getting to know people quickly is easy when you are acting and performing with them. Making up a story, pretending to be a character or an animal, taking part in a dance or song together, and sharing laughter are friendly things to do.

LETTING FRIENDSHIPS DEVELOP

Asking everybody to sit together in a circle or a group is enough to encourage some children to choose friends to sit next to and giggle with. Others will neither need nor want this at first. Allowing children to sit with their carers can give them the confidence to join in, but always ask them to sit within the circle and not behind it or some distance away, emphasising the social situation of friends coming together to share a drama class. Gradually encourage children to sit closer to each other and to choose their own places, sensitively ensuring that no particular children are the ones always chosen or never chosen as the 'friends' that others wish to sit next to.

Gradually decrease the amount of direction that you offer to the group at certain times, as you feel that they are gaining in social confidence. Allow short breaks for children to chat and laugh with each other, or just to exchange friendly looks and smiles. Don't talk all the time! Take a few moments to find a CD, a book or another prop, or wait before selecting a track on a music player, if you sense that some children would like to speak to each other and others would like to relax for a moment before concentrating on another new dramatic task.

There may be times when children would like to tell you about something important to them. This may be a happy or traumatic event in their lives or something that they presently find interesting. Try to make available various short 'time slots' during which this kind of talking could be appropriate. If they only want to talk to you, it may need to be before or after the session. But, if it is something they would like to share with the whole group, everybody might enjoy listening after each child has been introduced, or after a busy action song, or just before a story is read.

It is important to encourage all children to understand that they should want to listen to their peers and take an interest in what they have to say and that they should feel able to share their own observations and events with the group and expect that others will listen to them in return. They may then work towards early learning goals in the prime areas of Communication and Language (Speaking) and Personal, Social and Emotional Development (Managing feelings and behaviour).

If a recent event or experience has affected several or all of the children in the group, they may want to tell you about it. Encourage them to share the telling of a story, asking questions and prompting as necessary to display the correct level of interest but not altering or directing the way the story is told. Gently remind more confident children that others would like to speak too and ask them to wait for a few seconds from time to time. Invite quieter or more timid children to volunteer their opinions and ask others to listen to them. Taking part in a group conversation is a valuable skill to learn, which some children will find easier than others. The aim is to develop confidence in knowing when would be an appropriate moment to speak or to listen and expecting that others will observe the same standards. Once this confidence is established, taking part in conversations becomes enjoyable.

Try to think of events in your own life that the children could relate to and model general conversation for them to imitate. They may enjoy hearing about your children, pets, holidays, trips, birthday presents, minor mishaps, events and treats. They need to understand that adults also inhabit a less than perfect world and have to cope with life and other people every day; they have the same range of feelings and emotions as when they were younger, but have merely learned more self-control and do not always make their feelings so obvious.

Show children that you can feel wonder and amazement, joy, sadness, anger and understanding and encourage them to do the same, expressing themselves both verbally and non-verbally but with appreciation of others' needs and feelings. This will help to cement a relationship between you and enable you to work together productively.

You will need to become aware very quickly of which children achieve more and are less disruptive to the group if they are directed towards activities separately. It may be appropriate to seat them away from each other, but avoid always allowing them to sit beside you or paying them extra attention that could be interpreted as rewards by the other children, or the unwanted behaviour may be copied! A new or timid child may be afraid of interacting with more boisterous children at first and will make greater progress if placed beside calmer class members. Getting to know the abilities and personalities of every member of the group is crucial.

IN A NURSERY OR SCHOOL SETTING

Children's friendships may be well developed or forming rapidly and practitioners will be monitoring and assisting this. Drama sessions may offer extension activities that further develop children's abilities to relate to each other and work together. Be guided by the observations of each child's teacher or key person and discuss together, out of the children's hearing, relationships that you would like to encourage or discourage, in order to work consistently for the benefit of all children.

IN PRIVATE CLASSES

Some children may attend a class with friends and others may know nobody when they first join the group. Some parents and carers bring their children to classes because they are hoping to make new friends, but others are very busy people and are only looking for the drama experience. Encourage new friendships to form if you see opportunities for them, but be aware of how constructive or otherwise the relationships may eventually be for the families. Explain to children that it can be fun to have special friends that you only see at drama sessions and would not otherwise have met at all.

If parents and carers stay, they will see relationships for themselves and monitor them as they wish. If they leave their child with you, they may want to ask you about friends that their child mentions between classes. Parents and carers have a right to know about the people that their children associate with, but you must be professional and not give out confidential information or details on any child or family. If you are asked to disclose

FIGURE 4.1 New friendships can develop as children act and dance together

information or contact details, you must first ask the other family's permission, or introduce the families to each other and let them make their own decisions.

GAMES AND ACTIVITIES

With support, children can form pairs and small groups during action songs, dancing and listening games and progress at their own pace, as they explore themes and ideas from their own knowledge and environment. This contributes to learning objectives within the specific area of Understanding the World (The world).

ACTIVITIES TO ENCOURAGE SOCIAL INTERACTION

- Rowing an imaginary boat.
- Throwing and catching an imaginary ball.
- Riding on an imaginary seesaw.
- Taking turns to describe what you built or found, saw or chose.
- Playing ring games.

- Dancing freely to music with a partner or in a ring of three or four children.
- Dancing with a partner and helping each other to freeze or sit down when the music stops.
- Searching or digging for imaginary items of treasure and bringing them back to share with the group at random.
- Creating an imaginary sandcastle or brick tower as a whole group or within smaller groups, finding items to use and helping it to balance.

Encourage children to create their own sound effects to enhance songs, rhymes and stories using their hands and feet, their bodies, their voices or percussion instruments. Offer and demonstrate a few simple examples to explain the activity, such as stamping feet to indicate marching soldiers, hissing sounds to create snakes or bells being shaken for telephones or doorbells.

Support them as they work together, as a large group or in smaller groups, to think of new effects and try them out. Provide maracas, drums and sticks and challenge them to create different sounds for rain falling

FIGURE 4.2 Encouraging small groups to create sound effects using percussion instruments

lightly and more heavily and then a thunderstorm. Suggest that people might run home quickly through the rain or enjoy splashing in puddles and wait to see which children think of using their hands or feet to make those sounds.

Encourage the groups to use their sound effects as they sing songs such as 'I Hear Thunder' and 'Incy Wincy Spider'.

DEGREES OF INTERACTION

Some people are happy to follow the crowd, while others prefer to be different. Children must learn to judge when one type of behaviour would be more appropriate than another, through adults setting good examples and offering opportunities for them to experience social situations. While those who think for themselves, develop ideas and embrace imagination are important to our world, we all need to understand when it is necessary to conform to an accepted social standard and learn to do this as we grow up. (While a toddler might be forgiven for throwing a toy across a doctors' waiting room or shouting in a library, an older child would be frowned upon by others sharing the facility and an adult would be asked to leave!)

Somewhere between the age of 3 and the age of 6, most children learn how to wait their turn for an adult's attention; how to listen to their friends as well as talk to them; how to answer questions; how to wait quietly in a queue, shop or waiting room; how to ask politely for what they would like and to say thank you when they receive it; and to accept that they cannot always have exactly what they want immediately, or even at all. These are aspects of the early learning goal for the prime area of Communication and Language (Understanding).

Children need these important skills to ensure that others will like them, listen and talk to them and invite them to join in with games and activities. The child who shouts above all his classmates, can never stand or sit still, never listens to instructions and expects others to make allowances but never does so in return, will be the one in trouble at school and in clubs and in danger of being excluded from friendships, birthday parties, outings and treats.

A child should be praised for thinking up or using original ideas that fit within a context, but one who copies others is also learning to conform socially. The child who seems completely unaware of what others are doing and unable to copy or join in with the activity is the one who should give cause for concern. A lack of social interaction coupled with a lack of any desire for it could make a practitioner suspect that a child has a degree of disability or special need. The child who does not respond, listen or speak may have a hearing loss, while the child who makes a lot of noise but refuses to sit down near to any other person or to move on to a different activity may have a communication difficulty, such as autism.

TACTILE EXPERIENCES

Through drama, children learn to understand their own bodies and what they can do with them. They may work on action songs that involve pointing to or moving various parts of the body and learn to walk, run, jump, hop, skip, tiptoe, 'skate', take giant steps or tiny ones, dance, creep, crawl, roll, stop and freeze. They will become more confident in using their bodies to interact with others in the group, both by touching each other and by avoiding collisions when dancing or moving around. These are important early learning goals within the prime area of Physical Development (Moving and handling).

It is a good idea to offer a group song at the end of a session, which involves everybody holding hands in a circle. If the same song is used at each class, the children will get used to the actions and be prepared to hold hands at the appropriate time. They will probably not be ready to do this at the beginning of a class, but may do it easily by the middle of the session if a well-known ring game is introduced. Reinforcing this at the end allows children to go away from the session with the warm feeling that they have been working with friends and makes them more eager to return.

If a child is not yet ready to hold hands with other children, you could try temporarily placing an adult at one or both sides of the child, or inviting the child to move forwards (not backwards to feel excluded by the circle of hands) and to sit within the circle while others hold hands around and behind, or sitting the child in front of you while you hold the hands of those beside you. Provide the same opportunity to join hands at each session and offer praise, but make no fuss as each child finds the courage to participate. Don't have set places for children within the circle, but ask them all to come and join in by sitting or standing in any space available, so that they are beside different friends each time. Your ultimate aim is for every child to be happy to take the hands of the children on either side, whoever they are.

Some people naturally touch and hug others often, while some never get that close to anyone outside their immediate family. Some children come from families who pick them up and cuddle them a lot, while some maintain their relationships through talking or doing things together. Explain to the group that holding hands or dancing together is just something that is fun to do and only lasts as long as the song or activity.

Whenever you would like to encourage further social interaction between the members of your group, or you need a quiet activity to calm the children, you could spend a few minutes seated in a circle to play a simple drama game. Pretend that you are holding a tiny animal, or any object of your choice, and whisper to the children that you would like to pass it around for everybody to see, but that it is very easily frightened by quick movements and noises, then pass it around the circle from hand to hand. Encourage each child and adult in turn to take the imaginary item carefully, hold it for a moment and then pass it on, until it comes back to you.

GETTING IN AND GETTING OUT

Be at your most persuasive when asking all children to join in with the first and last activities, because the entering and leaving of any social situation are the hardest parts. They need to begin to learn and develop these skills as early as possible, to allow them plenty of time to practise them. Most people can do what they once thought of as 'scary' things once they feel confident of how to start and how to stop.

Chapter 5

Mime and expression

Very young children are naturally very expressive and will readily display their emotions for all to see, particularly when they are excited, displeased or upset! Learning to express themselves without sound or speech, through a variety of games and activities, can help them to develop a greater self-control, to communicate with others and to understand and empathise with other people's feelings.

Tell children that you are going to work on special acting without any talking or sound and that this is called . . . miming! After two or three sessions most of them will be able to finish the sentence for you, as well as recognise other mime situations and tell their families about mime. They will also come to understand that acting means one thing standing for another, just as it does in their role play, and begin to appreciate the meanings of words such as symbolic, action, sequence and expression. This makes important links between learning objectives in the prime area of Communication and Language (Speaking) and the specific area of Expressive Arts and Design (Being imaginative).

GAMES TO PLAY TO ENCOURAGE EXPRESSIVE MIME

Begin with a simple game of 'making faces'. Sit or stand in a circle or in two lines. Ask the children to show you a face and model it for them, making sure they can all see you clearly and understand that this is acting and pretending, so it should be exaggerated.

A range of expressions for faces alone can be taught, such as:

happy, sad, worried, frightened, tired, surprised, thinking, excited – and (the children's favourite) – cross!

Encourage the use of arms and hands to enhance expressions if children are ready:

- hands on hips or arms folded can emphasise being cross;
- hands to mouth can add to a worried or frightened look;
- rubbing eyes or covering a yawn goes well with a tired face;
- hands raised look surprised;
- a finger on a chin indicates thinking;
- clenched fists close to the body enhance an excited expression.

Younger children will enjoy making the same faces over and over again until they feel very sure of what each expression means and how it makes them feel. But, for the adults' sake, it is sensible to vary the order in which they are made. Have a selection of ten or twelve different expressions prepared and work on a different combination of four, six or eight in each session. This allows enough repetition for the children, without the adults becoming too bored to participate enthusiastically! Gradually ask the children to change their expressions more quickly as they become increasingly confident and proficient at remembering them.

Once a range of expressions have been introduced, discussed and practised and the children are familiar with them, play games such as:

Make the face I call out.

Guess which face I'm making and call out its name.

Copy the face I make and change it when I do.

Take turns to show us all your favourite expression.

Show your favourite expression to the person sitting next to you.

Some children will become confident enough to enjoy showing an expression to the whole group or making a face for the whole group to guess. Others will not be ready to do this until after the end of the EYFS. Only those who are ready to move on to this level of learning should be encouraged to do so, but children can become upset or lose confidence if they are not invited to join in, when they just did not want to jump up and down and shout out that they wanted to take a turn. Some children find it hard to understand exactly what is being asked in a whole group situation. It is best to offer each individual child the opportunity to do it and accept their response sensitively and without fuss whether they agree or refuse, repeating the offer at regular intervals.

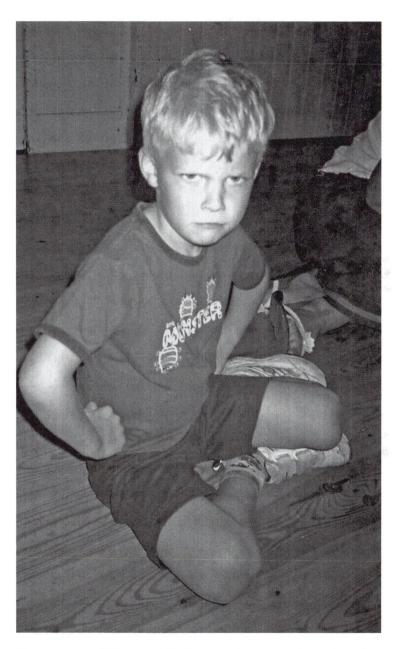

FIGURE 5.1 Children quickly learn to mime expressions – 'cross' being a favourite choice!

FIGURE 5.2 'Worried' is a dramatic expression that children enjoy using when acting out stories

Some children will agree to any new experience and happily try their best, not worrying about making mistakes, as long as they feel secure and supported within the learning situation. Some will refuse at first, but watch others until they feel confident and then eagerly request their turn. Others will refuse for a term or longer, but still enjoy and learn from watching how other children approach the task in various ways. Recognising the type of person they are within a group situation and feeling comfortable with this is another important learning experience for a child. This can only come through practical experiences, where the support of sensitive and experienced practitioners can ensure that all children feel positive about themselves, whatever their abilities and talents.

Carefully praise one child for their abilities in expression and mime, another for their talent in dance and movement and another for their original ideas in speechwork, making it clear that we are all differently able but all good at something and each skill is equally valuable. The most useful praise is one that recognises a child's improvement in a skill they were struggling with or lacked confidence in, however slight the improvement, and any effort a child is making to overcome a difficulty or increase a proficiency.

USING THE WHOLE BODY FOR MIME AND EXPRESSION

Once they are used to making expressions with their faces, children can be encouraged to create more sophisticated mimes involving their whole bodies. Try mimes such as:

- seeing a friend and waving hello;
- feeling sad at having to say goodbye;
- asking your friend to come here;
- lifting a heavy box;
- pushing a heavy wheelbarrow;
- flying a kite;
- searching through a drawer or cupboard;
- knocking at a door;
- opening a door;
- splashing in a puddle;
- climbing a mountain;

- running down a slope;
- digging a hole;
- making and decorating a sandcastle;
- playing on a slide and a seesaw;
- putting on a coat, hat, scarf and gloves;
- making a snowman;
- rolling in a pile of leaves.

MOVING ON TO MIMING SEQUENCES, CHARACTERS AND STORIES

Make up simple story sequences and encourage children to participate in portraying the stories in mime, by asking questions and demonstrating actions of your own alongside them. A simple example could be:

- What might I look like if I was a very old person?
- And how might I walk?
- How might I move if I was feeling very tired and thirsty?
- How do you think I would feel if the rain fell on me?
- What might I need to use?
- How would I hold it?
- What would happen if the wind blew strongly?
- And then how would I feel if the sun came out?
- How would I feel when I got home at last?
- What would I do first when I got there?

Simple sequences that children can learn to perform from memory are:

- climbing stairs, putting on pyjamas, cleaning teeth, finding teddy and going to bed;
- digging a hole, planting seeds, watering seeds, sitting in sun, seeing seeds grow into flowers;
- fetching bricks in a wheelbarrow, mixing cement, building a wall or tower;
- putting on outdoor clothes;

- making footprints in snow, making a snowman;
- catching a train to the seaside, digging a sandcastle, swimming in the sea, taking a train home again;
- meeting a friend, playing on a swing, slide, seesaw and roundabout, saying goodbye.

Explain frequently that there are no right or wrong ways to mime a word or action. If another person understands what you mean, your mime is successful (and even if they don't, it may still be entertaining!).

It may be helpful and constructive for a group working together to agree on certain basic mimes to indicate frequently used words and actions, or it may be more appropriate for each individual to interpret them in their own way. Encourage all members of the group to be as inventive as they like and to share and discuss new ideas with others.

If you have children or adults with special needs or a degree of hearing loss within the group, or those who are not yet proficient in the language the lesson is conducted in, mime will be an area in which they can always participate on an equal level with everybody else.

If any sign language is known or used by a member of the group, it can be incorporated into mime activities. It is an excellent idea for any practitioner intending to use drama with young children to learn basic skills in one or more sign languages and be prepared to use them. Makaton is particularly appropriate for young children and easy to learn and use. It is designed to be used alongside speech and so may help those still learning the language to feel more confident in making themselves understood.

Begin with simple action songs and move on to miming characters and stories as the group grows in experience, confidence and proficiency. Most nursery rhymes can be acted out in mime, but many of them require lots of different actions following each other very quickly, so they are not always the simplest for use in mime.

Look out for children's songs that describe a particular action or project and offer lots of opportunities for repetition, such as songs about:

- building a house or a tower;
- digging the garden or field and planting seeds;
- sleeping and waking;
- working with various tools;

- driving or being various vehicles;
- moving as various animals;
- jumping, stamping, hopping, tiptoeing, etc.

It is a simple step from these sequences and songs to move on to acting out simple stories with lots of action and humour or phrases that are repeated often. Read or tell a story, using a book, poster or pictures and encourage discussion and group participation. Choose stories with lots of actions and humour or phrases that are repeated often. Include tales involving popular characters from children's books and television, as well as favourites such as: *We're Going on a Bear Hunt* by Michael Rosen and Helen Oxenbury (Walker Books), *Mr Gumpy's Outing* by John Burningham (Red Fox Books) and *Where the Wild Things Are* by Maurice Sendak (Harper Collins).

Challenge the children to re-tell the story in mime. This contributes to learning objectives within the specific area of Literacy (Reading), as they demonstrate understanding of what has been read. Work alongside them, performing appropriate actions and mimes and prompting them with cues, to ensure that they can move from the beginning of the story to the end without omitting a part that they would like to include. Always praise the group as a team at the end of this project, telling them what a good story they made together.

Share some traditional fairy tales with the children and support them in acting out the most well-known parts of the stories. Favourites may include: *The Three Billy Goats Gruff*, *Goldilocks and the Three Bears*, *The Three Little Pigs* and *Jack and the Beanstalk*. Encourage children to mime expressions or actions and ask others to guess the characters, such as a cross goat or bear, a fierce troll, wolf or giant or a scared pig or child.

The children will love it if you can supply appropriate character toys and speak to them, letting them whisper into your ear how clever they thought all the children were at acting and how pleased they are to have come, then bow and wave to the children before returning to their bag to have a sleep!

Visual aids of this kind can encourage the most timid and the most uncooperative children to participate and ensure that all children remember the story and activity well enough to recount it to family members or carers later. When children spontaneously talk about an activity and obviously remember it with enjoyment, adults can appreciate its value and the learning experience is enhanced for everybody.

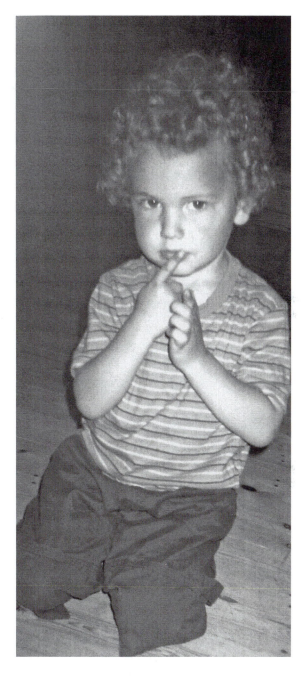

FIGURE 5.3 Children think deeply about new characters and stories that are introduced to them

■ **FIGURE 5.4** Children will begin to write and draw their own stories

Towards the end of the EYFS, some 4 and 5 year olds may begin to read books for themselves and acquire enough phonic knowledge to try to write and draw their own stories, working towards the early learning goals in the specific area of Literacy (Reading, Writing).

Teachers and practitioners should ensure that children have access to a variety of paper and mark-making tools from a very young age and are supported in their early attempts at representational drawings and emergent writing. As well as practising phonic sounds, early reading and correct letter formation, children must continue to experience a rich variety of stories and poems, throughout the EYFS and beyond.

Imagination and creativity will be enhanced and developed if children are encouraged to act out the stories they write and draw through role play or with puppets, combining early literacy skills with drama.

Chapter 6

Movement and dance

During the EYFS, children need time and opportunities to work, play and explore with their own bodies, so that they may develop good control and co-ordination in large and small movements and move confidently in a range of ways, safely negotiating space. Reinforcing these skills contributes to early learning goals within the prime area of Physical Development (Moving and handling).

BASIC MOVEMENT SKILLS FOR USE IN DRAMA

In order to act and portray characters and situations, children must feel confident that they can make their bodies show what they are thinking. In early sessions with any group, you must find out what stage each child has reached in the development of motor skills and offer them all opportunities to reinforce these and move on at appropriate levels. Basic skills to check include:

walking; running; jumping; hopping; skipping; stamping; galloping; tiptoeing; skating; spinning; climbing; balancing; dancing.

Very young children may not yet be able to hop or skip proficiently, but they can learn what the movements look and feel like by holding on to an adult or a wall for balance and trying to copy others who are willing to demonstrate. They will gradually come to understand the difference between galloping, which involves leading with the same leg throughout the movement, and skipping, which involves changing the leading leg with each step.

A skating movement means sliding feet across the floor and taking care with balance. A climbing movement means lifting legs and feet high with arms held up, as though on a ladder or mountain. Balancing can mean standing on one leg, walking along a string or a painted or imaginary line on the floor or assuming various dance or gymnastic positions. Dancing simply means moving to music in a rhythmic and enjoyable manner.

While learning and practising movements, discuss with the children the importance of physical exercise for good health. Acquiring an understanding of this is an early learning goal within the prime area of Physical Development (Health and self-care). Feeling able to control their own bodies well enough to move around among others safely and co-operatively, avoiding accidents and confusions, is essential for children's growing confidence and self-esteem. Children who are proficient at basic movement skills are also likely to be confident and accomplished when using play equipment such as climbing frames and tricycles, which is another health and safety bonus!

FREQUENT AND REGULAR MOVEMENT OPPORTUNITIES

Provide regular times during each day or week to practise movements. If children attend a setting on a sessional basis, ensure that each child has

FIGURE 6.1 Moving to music develops co-ordination skills

a chance to participate at least once a week. In a school reception class, children will have designated times for PE lessons, but they should have access to their own outdoor space for free flow play throughout most of each day, which can also be used for extra movement activities.

If children attend private classes, plan to develop new movement skills at a regular point in the class, preferably fairly early, when the children are settled but not tired. Begin with a warm-up song, then welcome everybody and offer a mime or acting activity to bring the group together. After this, the children will be ready and eager to use their whole bodies to move around and work on action songs, dances and gross motor skills. Adjust the length of this activity for a few weeks until you have decided at which point most children are happily tiring and ready to do something else and then follow it with a quieter activity, such as speaking a rhyme or listening to and acting out a story.

SAFETY AND CARE

Before letting children loose to set off around the room at random, establish some safety rules and give warnings about taking reasonable care. Demonstrate sensible behaviour and silly behaviour, so that even the youngest or least verbal child can understand the possible consequences of losing control. During quick movements, such as running or galloping, all children should be travelling in the same direction around the room and looking out for others all the time, to avoid collisions. During slow movements, such as tiptoeing or stamping, children may enjoy weaving around each other and this will help to make them more aware of the amount of space they need for their body to pass safely among a crowd of others. A remote control for your music player will prevent you from having to leave a circle of children or rush through a group of dancers or actors to turn music on or off.

We all need to have enough spatial awareness to negotiate a safe pathway before we can venture out into the streets without an adult's hand or a pushchair! The activities in this chapter particularly encourage children to achieve the early learning goals within the prime area of Physical Development (Moving and handling, Health and self-care).

Inevitably, within the early years, there are bound to be a few bumps and bruises occasionally. Young children do trip over their own feet and fall for no apparent reason when they are running or dancing. They will sometimes bump into each other, because they cannot yet be fully aware of their own movements and those of everybody else around them at the same time. They will gradually stop doing this as they absorb this stage of learning and move on. As long as only minor accidents occur, children may be easily comforted and will usually be eager to join in again within a few minutes.

IN PRIVATE CLASSES

Children in private classes must be discouraged from bringing food, drinks and toys into the working space during sessions, as these can become hazardous. A wet floor is slippery and so are biscuit crumbs or raisins scattered by a baby. A toy left on the floor can trip a child dancing by. Children can be fascinated by toys belonging to others and this can cause problems when a child is understandably reluctant to share a special item or a group is distracted by the charms of a friend's toy.

If possible, provide an adjoining room or separate space for babies to eat and play, or tactfully remind parents and carers to keep them to the sides of the room, on their laps or in pushchairs. Never allow a child to participate in a class holding food, a drink or a dummy. You may choose to allow children to hold their soft toys within a seated circle for speech-work or an action song, or to dance with them during a listening skills game such as 'Musical Statues', if you feel that they help the shyer children to speak up or join in. But, at all other times, it is best to have a special place for any toys from home to sit to watch the class and to be prepared to admire them and discuss them with children only before and after sessions.

IN SCHOOLS AND NURSERIES

Always observe the correct ratio of adults to children for the age group you are working with and include extra adults if they are available. Children with additional needs may require one-to-one adult support. Ideally a group should not consist of more than sixteen children working on drama at a time, except in a school, where the reception class may use the hall to access enough space and the children are working with the same classmates and adults on a daily basis.

The leader of an early years class should always be supernumerary, to avoid the session grinding to a halt because of one child becoming hurt or upset or needing to go to the toilet. This may not be possible in a reception class, as the class teacher will always be included in the ratio, but it becomes less important within a school because these children are moving towards the end of the EYFS and may practise greater independence and go to the toilet alone. Their teaching assistant will be used to dealing with all minor upsets within the class and there will also always be other adults available, who are close by and can be called upon to assist in any emergency.

ENCOURAGING SAFE BEHAVIOUR

Children who find it hard to move safely among a group or who become very excited and unable to maintain self-control can be encouraged to stand still and watch with a practitioner or parent for a few minutes and talk about how other children are managing to avoid each other, then to gradually join in while holding the adult's hand, until they feel able to try again alone. This process of asking a child to come out of a situation temporarily can be repeated whenever a child's behaviour becomes potentially hazardous. It should be seen as a part of the learning experience and not as a punishment, contributing towards learning objectives within the prime areas of Communication and Language (Understanding) and Personal, Social and Emotional Development (Managing feelings and behaviour, Making relationships).

Children who continue to deliberately push or bump into others or who scream and run wildly, even after repeated requests and warnings, will need to be temporarily removed from the situation. These children may need one-to-one adult assistance to learn to join in safely with the activity on future occasions and lots of praise each time they make movements in an acceptable manner.

Ring games can be an excellent way of teaching movements to a whole group and making everybody feel involved. Children and parents usually enjoy them and they can be a great way to cheer everybody up on a dull day; you will feel spirits rise as a 'party mood' takes over. However, these games can be limiting, place an emphasis on 'getting it right' and do not allow for much free expression, so it is best to keep a few favourite games for the beginning and end of sessions (and parties) and to use them sparingly at other times.

Do not be afraid to let the children go! Some sessions held in small rooms by inexperienced practitioners can involve children in copying a succession of words, actions and movements without ever moving out of a circle, for more than half an hour. This is not an ideal way for young children to learn. Children need to be able to set off on their own path around the room and try out their own ideas. The practitioner leading

FIGURE 6.2 Ring games can teach movements to a group and make everybody feel involved

the session needs to be able to watch each child individually and see that what they are doing is valuable; praising those developing greater skills, encouraging those trying something new and calming those becoming more excited than constructive. This requires experience and confidence, but when you are sure you know how your group of children is likely to react and behave and you believe that they will come back together when you offer the next activity, you will be able to facilitate their real learning experiences.

CHANGING THE FORMATION

While children thrive on repetition and familiar experiences, they are always willing to embrace new challenges and try out new activities, if they feel secure and supported within the situation and the setting. Young children can concentrate for extended periods of time if they are interested in what they are doing and enjoying exploring an activity, but, at other times, their attention span can be brief. It is important to change the activity frequently. Aim to offer a new project in an inviting manner at least every ten minutes in an early years drama class. Ensure that quieter work, such as speaking a rhyme or miming a sequence, alternates with noisier work, such as dancing, actions and movement.

Change the formation as often as the activity. Begin and end with a circle, to reinforce the idea of friendship and teamwork and to develop social skills. But ask the children to move from the circle into a line, then into their own spaces all over the room, then into two lines facing each other, then into a marching line with one behind another, then into a group to share a story and act it out. Avoid telling them exactly where to sit and stand, but, instead, show them how you use the space available and encourage them to follow you and develop their own ideas as they work.

Praise children for the creative use of space, such as crawling low along the floor or reaching high into the air when acting out a creature or character. Thank them when they use space sensibly for the good of those around them, such as making room for another child to join in, moving into a space left within a line or circle, or checking carefully before making a large or fast movement such as running or galloping. When children learn how to assess the space in a situation and move into and out of it constructively without upsetting or distracting others, they develop

FIGURE 6.3 Change the formation frequently, to work in lines, circles, groups and spaces

valuable skills in the prime areas of Physical Development (Moving and handling) and Personal, Social and Emotional Development (Making relationships, Managing feelings and behaviour).

PROMOTING UNDERSTANDING

Teach children the words we use to describe various types of movement and encourage them to learn them through making the movements themselves. When children feel and understand what it means to walk or run or tiptoe, they will not forget or mix up the words.

From walking age, children begin to learn a selection of movements with the support of adults or older children. Say, 'Let's all walk together' and play a piece of appropriate music, taking children by the hand and walking jauntily around the room. Then repeat the exercise with other movements. Having learned to walk quickly and slowly while they were 2 years old, children aged 3 and 4 will enjoy walking, running, jumping, stamping and dancing and be willing to explore a range of new movements.

Invite children to walk carefully along a real or imaginary string or chalked line on the floor, placing their feet one in front of the other, or to pretend that they are balancing along a wall that is only one brick wide. Suggest that they jump into puddles or piles of leaves and splash or kick their way through them, or leap from one stepping stone to another to cross a bog or a muddy field. Try the various movements both quickly and slowly and discuss which would be most effective in each situation.

Introduce drama props for exciting stimulation and challenge in movement and dance, such as hoops and ribbons on sticks. Offer the props to the children and ask for ideas of how they would like to use them. They may enjoy trying out a range of movements or just swirling around in time to some different pieces of music. But they might suggest that the hoops could be steering wheels or spiders' webs, or that the ribbons could be rainbows, fireworks, butterflies or snakes!

LEARNING THROUGH OPPOSITES AND CONTRASTS

Children love opposites and extremes. They like to imagine huge giants and tiny mice, running foxes and creeping snails, tall mountains and short grass, hard rocks and soft teddies, floating feathers and heavy bricks, balancing a sheet of paper on one hand or pushing a heavy wheelbarrow, digging a big hole and dropping in a tiny seed, splashing through a deep river or balancing on stepping stones.

Encourage this interest and exploit its learning potential through providing situations in which children can explore similarities and differences and act out contrasting movements and body shapes. Work on a different set of opposites in each session or each week of sessions, returning to each pair at intervals. Opposites that you could offer might be:

fast/slow; loud/quiet; big/small; tall/short; hard/soft; heavy/light; climbing up/slipping down; falling asleep/waking up.

Find two pieces of contrasting music, which suggest to you the appropriate opposites, or use two percussion instruments on which you can play contrasting sounds. Explain to the children that when they hear the first sound they should make the first type of movement and when they hear the second sound they should change their movement to fit. When first introducing this activity, demonstrate, join in and let them practise until you are sure they all understand. Then allow them plenty of space and let them work alone, while you play the music or make the sounds.

Emphasise that there is no one right movement for 'fast' or 'slow' – any type of movement that is fast or slow with any part of the body is correct and the movements could even be different each time the sound changes. Some children may choose to copy others while their confidence is still gradually developing and some small groups of children may choose to make the same movements as their friends, but independence and individual creativity should be encouraged and praised whenever seen.

Towards the end of the EYFS, children may be able to demonstrate their movements for the class to watch and imitate. This is a good way of rewarding children who have worked very hard and would love to show work to others, but avoid embarrassing children who do not like to be the centre of attention or they may deliberately not try so hard next time! Ensure all children are praised and that each child has a chance to show work to the class at some time over a term or similar period of sessions. Less confident children or those who prefer not to be in the limelight may be happy to show their work as a part of a small group rather than individually. Children who are working at an advanced level in movement skills may be ready to try working co-operatively with one or more friends to create a movement as a small group.

LISTENING SKILLS

Working with opposites and contrasts requires children to listen and react to what they hear. Listening skills are vitally important to learning objectives within the prime area of Communication and Language (Listening and attention). If children can listen carefully, take in and process information and then act upon it, they will be able to move forward in all other areas of development. Just as a child who has difficulties with hearing must receive help to avoid missing out on development, so too must a child who has difficulties with listening and understanding, since hearing words is not enough if you do not know what they mean or how they affect you.

FIGURE 6.4 Listening skills can be developed through games involving music, movement and dance

In dance and drama, listening skills can be easily practised in enjoyable ways. Games such as 'Musical Bumps' and 'Musical Statues' can be adapted to fit any theme in a session. Younger children love to dance to music and sit down when it stops. Slightly older ones love to freeze like statues. The game can become as complicated as you wish – try:

dance to the music and, when it stops, sit down, put your seat belt on and drive your car; or dance to the music and, when it stops, stand very still on one leg with one finger on your nose and the other hand on your head; or dance to the music and, when it stops, quack like a duck!

These games can be used to allow children to make a noise and use lots of space again after a quiet activity, or to allow them to move more gently after a boisterous action song. They require less concentration than learning a new skill or remembering the words of a song or rhyme, so are ideal to bring some light-hearted smiles and giggles back into the session. Young children are wonderful when they dance freely to popular music – the spontaneous movements they make with their bodies complement the mixture of concentration, expectation and glee on their faces – and few parents and practitioners can resist joining in with them!

DANCE

Formal dance training is available to children in a variety of different dance schools and groups and in some primary and nursery schools. Most dance teachers will accept children from the age of 3 or earlier and run special nursery or playdance classes for children under 5. As they grow older, the opportunities are endless: ballet, tap, jazz, disco, modern, street, gym dance, line dance, hip hop, etc!

The benefits of sharing an interest in dance with others in classes, learning correct techniques, taking exams, performing onstage and loyally pursuing an activity with other teachers and classmates, away from the weekly routine of school or nursery, can be tremendous. Dance is an excellent source of exercise, discipline, confidence and friendship for both boys and girls.

But not all children will be able to dance in their leisure time and not all will want to. Many will have different hobbies and many families do not have the time or the resources to make such a commitment for their children. All children should have the opportunity to explore dance as a part of their daily lives and education, along with sport, artistic and academic activities. Any rhythmic movement inspired by music or a beat can be called dance.

Chapter 7

Speech and language

We live in a world that relies totally on communication. Children need to be able to communicate with others without frustration, to enjoy creating and developing their own ideas and to understand and participate within any project as a member of a group. Clear speech and good language skills are an asset and acquiring, developing and practising them can be fun. The activities in this chapter contribute particularly to the achievement of the early learning goals within the prime area of Communication and Language (Listening and attention, Understanding, Speaking).

ENUNCIATING IN UNISON

Enunciation is the art of speaking clearly and precisely and something that all actors and singers work on. There are many sounds, chants and exercises used by adults to facilitate and maintain good enunciation, but young children can learn and practise their speech skills enjoyably through the saying of sentences, rhymes and songs together.

Gather the children into a group and tell them that you are going to do some 'special talking' together. Then explain to them that special talking is called 'enunciation'. Ask them to repeat the word with you. It is a word that young children love to say and chant and they find it no more difficult or unusual than a word such as 'ballet' or 'trampolining'. At each subsequent session, announce that it is time for 'special talking' and ask the children what it should be called. Within a few sessions, even the youngest 3 year olds will be calling out the answer.

Next, tell the children that when we all speak together at the same time it is called speaking 'in unison'. They usually find this even easier to remember and happily begin to tell the adults at home that they have been 'enunciating in unison' again today. This never fails to impress parents and other family members, but is, in fact, what young children naturally spend a lot of their time doing by choice when they are playing and are encouraged to do in order to learn facts, safety rules and new ideas.

Choose a selection of well-known nursery rhymes and work on a different one at each session. Ask how many children already know the rhyme, then invite them to listen to it carefully and either say it clearly yourself or play a good example of it from a children's CD. You may have to insist that they do listen quietly, as some of the more confident and enthusiastic children may want to join in immediately. Explain that it is important everybody in the group listens and thinks quietly first, as some may be hearing it for the first time and some rhymes are said differently in some verses by different people. After listening, agree on a version that everybody will use today.

Children enjoy 'warming their mouths up', by opening and shutting them, so invite them to do this first. Then ask the whole group to work together to enunciate in unison as they say the rhyme along with you. Maintain leadership of this, speaking slowly, clearly and loudly enough to encourage everybody to stay with you. It is a good idea to repeat the exercise at least once, speaking a little more quickly and with a little more volume as the group's confidence grows, but maintaining the rhythm and clarity.

RECOGNISING AND PREDICTING SPEECH

Children over 3 years always enjoy filling in words the leader 'forgets' and correcting 'mistakes'. This game requires good listening skills and builds on earlier activities involving contrasting sounds and reacting to silences.

First, introduce a well-known rhyme and allow the whole group to listen to it. Then let them practise enunciating it in unison. Once they are all confident of the rhyme and its words and rhythm, you can play slightly more advanced games. Tell the children that you would like to be able to say the rhyme again on your own, but that you are a bit forgetful and might need them to help you if you get stuck. Most will agree enthusiastically. Begin to say the rhyme again, but stop and look puzzled just before certain key words.

For example:

Baa baa black –
Have you any –

55

Yes sir, yes —
Three bags —

Encourage the children to fill in the missing words, praising and thanking them all, particularly those who respond most quickly or remember a word that most of the others cannot get. You are likely to hear some very amusing words at times with this game, as some children may have misheard certain words in favourite nursery rhymes, and it is fine to laugh with the children, so long as you never laugh at them or make them feel that what they said was wrong or silly.

When the group is proficient at filling in missing words, the game can be taken further. Instead of leaving puzzled gaps, speak the rhyme carefully but deliberately, say quite the wrong word at key moments and then pause when the children call out to you that you are wrong. For example:

Humpty Dumpty sat on a chair
Humpty Dumpty had a great jump
All the king's monkeys
And all the king's babies
Couldn't put Humpty to bed!

Young children love this game and through playing it, they are learning to listen and think critically, to distinguish right from wrong or likely from unlikely and to react quickly and confidently. It also makes them laugh, work as a team and enjoy the session.

TAKING CUES

When children fill in missing words or replace incorrect words, they are taking cues. Whenever you feel that the children are ready to absorb more new vocabulary, tell them that that is what they are doing. Ask them if they would please listen for the 'cue', which is what another person says or does just before they should speak, and then 'take their cue' and speak the correct word or line at the correct time.

Once they understand and have practised this, children aged 4 and 5 should be able to play at 'passing the rhyme around'. Ask them to sit in a circle with you, so that they can easily see when it will be their turn. Start the game by saying one line of a rhyme. Ask the child seated beside you to say the next line and the child seated beside him to continue. If the rhyme is short and ends before each player has taken a turn, it should be said again from the beginning, the first line following on immediately after the last line. Try this with various rhymes of different lengths, passing around the circle in both directions and with children seated in different places at each session.

When each child has spoken and the rhyme reaches its starting point again, either say the last line(s) yourself or suggest that everybody says them together. Then praise the children for taking their cues so well and enunciating so clearly. You can now explain that this was, of course, not enunciating in unison, it was enunciating individually.

If any children are unable or unwilling to speak up when it is their turn, it does not help to put pressure on them to do so. Allow enough seconds for natural hesitation, thinking or the summoning of courage, then ask each child by name whether they know the next line. If they don't know the lines but would like to speak, gently remind them of the words and then allow them their turn and praise them for achieving the enunciation. If they do know the lines but are not prepared to speak out, ask whether they would like to speak with you or with other children. If not, say the line yourself and pass on to the next child without any further comment. Give these children the same chance to participate at each session and they will suddenly do so one day when they feel ready and confident enough.

PLAYING WITH LANGUAGE

Enjoy rhymes with children and encourage them to think about and be sure that they understand what they are saying. If you use the rhyme 'Jack and Jill', ask them: 'What is a pail? What do we more usually call it now? Was it just sitting on the hill waiting? How did they get the water into it? Did Jack wear a crown? So was he a prince, then, or a king? What would your Mummy use if you bumped your head, instead of vinegar and brown paper?'

If you share 'Little Miss Muffet' with your group, ask: 'What do you think a tuffet was? What was curds and whey? Can you think of anything you might eat that would be like curds and whey? Did she eat them in a sandwich, or with a knife and fork, or in a bowl with a spoon? Was she frightened because the spider jumped out at her suddenly, or because he was so big, or because she didn't like spiders at all? Do you like spiders? Have you ever had one sit down beside you? Would it make you run away or would you be pleased?'

ACTING OUT

Once you have spoken a rhyme, children will welcome the opportunity to act it out, especially if it is usually sung and you have a good version of it available on a CD or DVD to act and sing along to. Discuss together how to create the various characters and portray what they do and how they feel, then fit actions and mimes to the song, singing along as much as possible. Nursery rhymes are usually sung quite quickly, so be prepared to act out a whole sequence in a few seconds and stress that this is part of the fun of this particular activity. It is a good idea to find or make a recording of the song sung at least two or three times, not just once, as your rapid actions may otherwise pass in a blur and the children may not feel satisfied that they really did act out the rhyme.

Offer opportunities for children to further develop their imaginations and character acting skills after sharing stories and rhymes.

Ask them individually:

If you were Daddy or Mummy Bear, what would you say to Goldilocks when you found her in your house?

■ **FIGURE 7.1** Children enjoy creating characters and actions to fit favourite songs and rhymes

If you were Snow White, what would you say to the seven dwarfs when the prince woke you up?

If you were the sorcerer's apprentice, what spell would you use to try to stop the brooms bringing more water?

If you were the hare, how would you feel when the tortoise won the race?

If you were Old Mother Hubbard, what would you do when you found that there were no bones left in your cupboard for your hungry dog?

If you were the dish, how would you make the spoon want to run away with you?

PROJECTION OF THE VOICE

If you have a stage or designated area that you use for performing to an audience, children will be able to practise speaking, singing and cue taking there. Explain to them that enunciation makes up half of the important way we speak onstage. The other half comes from being able to project your voice to an audience, so that they can hear you clearly even if they are some distance away. By the age of 4, children should be able to grasp the idea of sound waves coming out of their mouths, hitting the wall at the back of the hall or room and falling down over the audience. Teach children to take a breath and push their voices out, speaking slightly more slowly and slightly more loudly than usual, but not shouting, and remembering to enunciate.

If children are speaking in unison, encourage them to maintain a sensible speed and not to slow down to wait for each other until the speech becomes a mournful chant! If they are speaking individually, encourage them each to find their own comfortable speed and style of speaking and to take cues confidently. It is possible for children to learn to do this and to enjoy the experience of performing to an invited audience of their own families and friends from the age of 3 years, provided that they have an adequate level of support and encouragement from practitioners throughout the experience and that the whole event is carefully planned and monitored to run smoothly but flexibly, putting the needs of the children first.

In regular group sessions, allow time for conversations and discussions, as these enrich language development. Young children's vocabularies

FIGURE 7.2 Teach children to project their voices by pushing them out to the audience

increase at an astonishing rate and their pronunciation and understanding of words can only improve through practice. Model correct speech yourself at all times, taking care to enunciate clearly and to project your own voice to lead activities, rather than shouting. When children become noisy and excited and it is time to change to a quieter activity, one loudly projected request to stop and gather around, followed by soft speech or whispers to those who come to join in is very effective in calming and refocusing the group.

Naturally demonstrate, through your own example, different forms of correct speech for different situations. Enunciation during rhymes, projection onstage and conversational language used when chatting within a group, require subtle differences in approach that children can only learn and absorb through planned and shared experiences with caring and interested adults. Listen carefully to children's spontaneous speech and make appropriate comments and replies, proving your interest and demonstrating the correct 'give and take' nature of conversations for children to imitate.

SPECIAL OR ADDITIONAL NEEDS

A child who has a hearing and/or a speech impairment may have difficulty with some speech and language activities, but you should aim to make them accessible to everybody. One-to-one support may be needed in some cases and this could be provided by an adult or, sometimes, by a caring and sensible child.

Chanting and singing will aid the development of enunciation and encourage a child to form words more quickly to maintain a rhythm. They can also help a child who feels isolated to feel accepted and welcomed within a group, as singing is an excellent social experience, which encourages people to come together, regardless of their similarities or differences.

All attempts to communicate should be praised and encouraged. Even a child with little coherent speech should feel able and eager to join in, through sounds or signing or a combination of the two. Familiarise yourself with particular signs that a specific child in your care uses, but accept a parent, carer, key person or teaching assistant as a translator if this will help a child to communicate more effectively. Signing can include a rich use of language and vocabulary and allow a child to display their intelligence and imagination despite a disability.

Children who have English as an additional language can benefit from all drama activities, but will particularly increase their understanding and use of the language through listening to stories, chanting rhymes, singing songs and matching mimes and actions to words. They may also participate in sessions with an adult or another child to assist in translation as necessary. Or, in private classes, a child may even attend with a parent or relative who has little experience of English and become the translator in their turn.

Chapter 8

Rhythm and singing

From birth, babies enjoy being sung to and listening to music. As they grow up, children enjoy singing along to favourite tunes and joining in with familiar songs and rhymes with families and friends, teachers and carers and groups of other children. While children must have quiet times for rest and concentration and should not be distracted by the constant background noise of a television or radio, children's songs or music that is easy to listen to can often provide a calmer and happier atmosphere for free play than complete silence. Children may then choose to sing or dance along at times, or just listen as they build, create and interact with each other.

Although many parents will share songs with their children at home, they will also expect them to experience singing and rhythm activities within their peer group in an early years or school setting, or take them to private groups and classes especially for this experience. The activities in this chapter contribute particularly to the early learning goals within the specific area of Expressive Arts and Design (Exploring and using media and materials, Being imaginative).

INCLUDE SOME FAMILIAR SONGS

During their early years, many children will experience some songs with their families or regular carers. Try to find out which songs are already favourites and consider using some of them within your singing sessions, as well as the new material that you plan to introduce. If they are not able to remember any songs by name, guess at some and begin to sing or play them. It will be obvious which children are familiar with them, as they will smile in recognition and begin to join in with the singing or bounce along to the rhythm.

Nursery rhymes are introduced to children because they are fun to learn and sing together and easy to remember, although some of the words are old-fashioned and some of the rhymes unusual. Sometimes they can demand quite a wide voice range to sing well, but young children will not worry about getting the tune perfectly correct and will happily join in with their own approximations. They are also an important part of our history and heritage and a part of childhood that has been shared by many generations. Many other simple songs have become popular over the years, often with repetitive actions and choruses that relate to children's everyday experiences.

You may prefer to sing unaccompanied, or you may enjoy singing along with recorded music or interesting backing sounds. Never be afraid to add harmonies and variations to simple tunes and to explore a wide variety of songs. Children and adults enjoy listening to somebody sing for pleasure and a live performance, either unaccompanied or with a backing track, is a treat.

If you do not sing confidently, you may feel happier with the support of a simple recorded version of a song, or you may find it easier to start a song and encourage the children to take over with their voices, just maintaining the timing and rhythm with them, to keep them singing together. Remember that young children are not judgemental and although they may come to realise that they really enjoy listening to particular adults sing or feel especially inspired by them, they will appreciate everybody's efforts and never decide that somebody 'can't sing'. It is important that all adults involved with the children understand this and ensure that no child ever feels or says 'I can't sing' because somebody has said such a thing to them or within their hearing. You don't have to have a voice of a standard to perform a solo in a concert to enjoy singing as a group activity!

Using some familiar songs and rhymes makes it likely that the adults in the group will know them and feel confident enough to join in and encourage the children immediately. They are then more likely to learn new ones easily. It is extremely useful for any group or class leader, practitioner or teacher to have a repertoire of familiar songs and rhymes that the children enjoy singing and chanting together. They can be used during singing sessions, or at any time to bring a drifting group back together or to warn children that it is about to be time for the next part of a setting's routine, such as a mealtime.

TEACHING NEW SONGS

When you have chosen a new song that you would like to introduce to the children, tell them about it with enthusiasm and introduce it at a time when they are receptive to learning something new – not when they are tired or hungry, or have just spent an extended period concentrating on other new or demanding activities or have been sitting still for too long. Explain a little about the song first, but avoid complicated background information, which would be inappropriate for this age group. The children might be interested to know if a particular character or animal or type of person usually sings the song, if it tells a story, describes a feeling or reminds us of some simple rules. Always tell them that you like the song and would like to share it with them and hope that they will like it too.

Either play a recorded version of the song to the children or sing it to them, unaccompanied or with an instrument if you play one. The ability to play a piano or a guitar can enhance a singing experience for the group, as it allows the teacher to sing along. Instruments that must be blown can be used to help to teach a tune in the early stages of learning a song, but young children are unable to sing along to them, as their ability to maintain rhythm and timing varies too much without a strong leading voice.

It is best to sit close to the children and maintain eye contact with them while singing and playing. Percussion instruments, such as tambourines, small drums, bells or maracas, can be very helpful in establishing a strong rhythm, but be aware that if you play one the children will all want to play one too, so be prepared to arrange a session with instruments for them or to pass the instrument around and let them all take a turn.

If a colleague or a parent offers to play the piano, guitar or a similar instrument on some occasions, while the class leader sings with the music for the children, this can be very successful for the sharing of new songs and rhymes that the children will learn to sing. However, you will still need some recordings for dance music and listening games. It is ideal if children can experience a mixture of live and recorded music.

Unless the song is very short, teach a part of it at a time, starting with the simplest part or a chorus that repeats. When the children have listened to the song, sing a line at a time for them and ask them to sing it back to you or sing it again with you. Repeat any line that is hard to learn until the majority of the singers can manage it. When they have mastered four lines or one simple verse or chorus, put it all together and sing it as a group. After working on each new part, return to the chorus or the part you all know well, to ensure that the children's self confidence remains

FIGURE 8.1 If a pianist is available, children can experience both live and recorded music

high. Give lots of praise for the effort and progress they are making and the good sounds that are being achieved.

Introduce a new song over more than one session and allow children to 'warm up' and 'cool down' with more well known ones, working on the new one in the middle of a singing session. It will gradually become so familiar that the children will no longer see it as a new song. Once they all know it well, it is fun to remind them of how short a time ago they did not know it at all. It is then time to introduce another new song and ask the children to remember how easily they learned the previous one. This means that each new song is likely to be approached with a greater and greater confidence, as they begin to realise the potential learning ability at their command. If children firmly believe that they can do something, they usually can!

FAVOURITES

Note which songs are particular favourites with the children and return to them just often enough to make sure that they remain favourites – not the songs we have all become bored with! Children enjoy taking turns to choose a song and may even like to sing a part of their favourite song to the rest of the group before everybody sings it together. If you are going to encourage this, do make sure that turns are taken fairly and that each child is offered the opportunity to choose or perform within a suitable time period. It is better to look at your group and ask one or more children by name to select a song than to ask 'Who would like to choose a song for us?' Open ended questions and offers to this age group result in the loudest, boldest and most confident children taking a turn almost every time, while quieter or less confident children, or those who take a little longer to think about the question, may always be overlooked and never develop the desire to lead or even participate fully.

Some suggestions of suitable nursery rhymes and popular children's songs are included within the example drama session plans at the end of the book (see Appendices 1 and 2).

IN A NURSERY OR SCHOOL SETTING

You will usually be able to keep all your resources and materials in an appropriate room or area and use them as you wish. Although you will have planned your sessions and may be bringing in resources of your own, favourite songs should be available to you whenever you need them and whenever you can be flexible within your timetable.

If you are working on a theme, but you suddenly remember a song that will fit a particular child's present interest or enthusiasm, you should aim to introduce it quickly, respond to the interest and allow it to develop further before it wanes. Any interest may be shared with others of the peer group and can become the beginning of a stimulating topic for the group to explore. Songs, tunes and pieces of music can often be found quickly using iPods or the internet and played through speakers attached to computers, laptops, MP3 players or iPod docking stations, if these facilities exist within the setting.

IN PRIVATE CLASSES

Each session will be carefully planned in advance and only the appropriate resources will be available at each one, but it should still be possible to be a little flexible. If a child or parent requests a particular song that has become a favourite, perhaps from a previous term, you will probably have to say that you don't have it with you or can't fit it in today, but that you will try to include it in a session soon. There should always be room for flexibility within your planned themes and activities to respond to a child's area of specific interest or enjoyment as soon as possible, either by adding an extra item or swapping it for one that can as easily be used at another point in the future. Anything that makes a child or family feel special and valued by the class leader is important.

Choose songs that suit your range and preferred type of singing and perform each number confidently to your audience. There can be no greater encouragement to join in than a good singer happily and confidently leading and sharing a good song. You will often find that some of the adults have chosen to go to musical drama classes with their children because they enjoy singing themselves. They may also have good voices and be thrilled at the opportunity to use them along with you each week. Consider which new songs you could introduce that would be interesting and challenging to them as well as to the children.

When parents, grandparents, nannies and childminders spontaneously tell you how much fun they are having and ask where they can find copies of some of your songs to listen to at home, you know that you are getting it right. There is absolutely no need for young children's activities to be boring for the adults involved. Since it is the adults who must make the commitment to attending regularly and paying for the classes, it is sensible to ensure that they will be glad to do so. Special times that allow adults and their children to share and develop their skills together are valuable for their relationships, as well as for the learning that takes place.

BUSY TIMES AND QUIET TIMES

Alternate busy action songs, boisterous dance numbers and ring games with quieter songs and the chanting of rhymes. Children need a variety of opportunities to find and explore their voices. It can be fun to include work on opposites and contrasts within singing activities.

Ask the children to sing:

- as loudly as they can and then as softly as they can;
- in a jerky voice and then in a smooth voice;
- in a voice that gets gradually louder or gradually softer;
- in a cross voice or a pleased voice;
- in a character's voice – a baby, an old person, an angry troll, a lion, a snake, etc.

67

If you think the children are ready to learn more describing words, then offer them 'piano and forte', 'staccato and legatto', 'crescendo and diminuendo' as you work on them. Some songs specifically teach children about 'loud and soft' or 'happy and cross'. Many others can be adapted by an experienced practitioner to do so.

SONGS TO TEACH IMPORTANT LESSONS

Because singing is an enjoyable and team-building activity, it is the ideal medium for teaching other lessons. Singing along is one of the easiest ways to plant words, numbers, phrases and ideas in the memory. Music, singing and rhythmic chanting have been used extensively in the teaching of modern languages, historical facts and times tables to older children.

Acting out words as they are sung further reinforces messages. There are many CDs and recordings available containing songs that cover every aspect of care and learning for a young child. If you would like to remind them of anything from 'feeling special' to 'saying please and thank you' or 'being a good friend', you should be able to find a song to suit the situation. Young children can also enjoy and learn from singing songs in other languages, especially if they are languages spoken by families attending the setting.

RHYTHM

The art of hearing, understanding and responding to rhythm involves other activities too. Even people who are determined that they cannot or will not sing, can tap out a rhythm, or play instruments very successfully, or dance beautifully or move in a rhythmic way. Children need opportunities to explore rhythm separately from speech and singing and should be encouraged to develop skills and confidence in this area.

Moving to a beat played on a percussion instrument or to music allows children to hear and feel a rhythm and respond to it in a natural way. By the age of 3 or 4, most children should be able to listen to a rhythm and recognise when a walking movement would fit better than running, or when marching would be more appropriate than tiptoeing, or how fast or slow a jumping or hopping movement should be. Dancing freely to music of many different types will allow children to try out new ways of expressing themselves and develop the ability to fit their own movements to the rhythm they hear.

Playing along to songs with a variety of percussion instruments also develops abilities in rhythm, provided that the children are encouraged to listen and think about what they are hearing and singing. Songs involving clapping or hammering, stamping or marching tend to have very strong rhythms that can be easily recognised and copied, as do nursery rhymes. Demonstrate for children how to say or clap a rhythm and then repeat it with the instrument. Play and sing along with them, leading strongly with both your instrument and your voice. Allow them to practise as many times as they like. Return to familiar songs frequently and praise children who make efforts to emulate what they hear with a variety of instruments at each session. This activity must be led firmly and confidently by the adult, to keep children on task and ensure that some learning can take place. Free play with instruments may be offered as a separate activity at another time.

Children nearing the end of the EYFS may be able to extend their work on rhythm to create whole songs or tunes as a group. They could sit in a circle or a line and take turns to clap or play a small part of the song each, taking their cues and moving on from each other as they might have learned in speech and language activities. Or they might create a short performance of a well known or made up rhythm, working co-operatively within a very small group, and show it to their classmates.

Children who are working at an advanced level may like to copy a rhythm that you play, clap or stamp for them, or play, clap or stamp the rhythm of a song for you and the rest of the group to identify. They may even move on to copying and guessing rhythms within pairs or small groups independently, without your direct supervision or leadership, or choose to bring this into their own play at other times.

Use lots of number rhymes and songs and create rhythm activities including a different numbers of beats, in order to develop counting and problem solving skills that contribute to learning objectives within the specific area of Mathematics (Numbers).

Try dividing the class into two halves or smaller groups, each with adult support, and asking them to take turns to make sounds and echoes. When the children are proficient at copying the numbers of claps and stamps in rhythmic beats, challenge one group to close their eyes or look away while they listen to the sounds made by the other, then to look back and repeat what they heard, guessing how the different sounds were made.

Draw children's attention to the numbers of beats that are repeated within certain rhymes and how the timing of them can make the tune change even when the numbers are the same.

FIGURE 8.2 Advanced work on rhythm can involve clapping and stamping the beats of a song for others to copy or guess

In the beginning of one nursery rhyme, we hear:

Three blind mice, three blind mice,
see how they run; see how they run

There are three beats twice, followed by four beats twice.
In another song, we hear:

Pat a cake, pat a cake, baker's man,
bake me a cake as fast as you can

There are three beats in each phrase, but the first beat is slower in the third phrase. In all of the other phrases they are of the same length, but there is an extra beat at the end of the sixth phrase.

Although children aged 3 and 4 years will not be able to put these discoveries into words and may be confused by a verbal explanation, they will be able to hear, feel and understand the differences between the beats and the rhythms of the rhymes or tunes and learn to clap them for themselves.

AN EXTENSIVE REPERTOIRE

A crucial resource for any practitioner working in drama or music with young children is the knowledge of and the ability to remember, find and use a vast number of varied musical numbers. Sometimes you will plan what to use over an extended period (long-term planning), and sometimes you will develop ideas as you work on topics and see which areas interest and stimulate the children (medium-term planning). But there will also be times when you see how to enhance provision with an appropriate song, or you need to provide a five-minute constructive and enjoyable activity for the whole group, or you need to bring your group together to re-focus but they are too wriggly for a quiet story (short-term planning).

Collect songs from everywhere, all the time. If you hear a song that immediately suggests a use to you, or that you think you might like to use in the future, always find out what it is and arrange to buy or borrow a copy of it. If themes, ideas or songs come into your head at an unusual moment, write them down as soon as you can and look carefully at your notes later. This may mean that your planning is suddenly almost completed for a future term.

It is possible to find songs to fit a theme or to find a theme to fit songs. Never discard any song that you have used already or that you think you might not use after all. They take up almost no space – keep them all in case. You might suddenly find the perfect use for a song years after you collected it, or be able to exchange one with another practitioner who has different ideas or is working with a different age group.

If you have literally thousands of songs at your fingertips – in a neat array of clearly labelled CDs, or on an iPod or in a computer, as well as many in your head and on the tip of your tongue – you can be confident that you will always be able to plan well-structured musical, rhythmic and dramatic learning, or provide some constructive fun, with no notice at all.

Chapter 9

Taking turns

Children need to learn how and when to take turns with others. As adults, they will need this ability in order to speak in conversations, form queues in shops, wait for buses, sit in waiting rooms until they are called for appointments and find appropriate ways to achieve their desires without upsetting other people. Those who 'jump queues' or continuously interrupt with their own views and never listen to anybody else, find themselves without friends or the career and life possibilities they could have had if they were more able to make themselves acceptable to the majority.

Children in the early years see themselves as the centre of the world and have no concept of others having equal rights or of the need to learn to share and take turns with them. But they are capable of learning, provided they have lots of opportunities to practise the required skills and lots of positive encouragement, reminders and reinforcements from adults and older children. Drama provides many varied opportunities for taking turns and a good practitioner will make the most of all of them as they arise.

WAITING FOR CUES

Allow children to choose where to sit or stand and then ask them to look carefully at the people who are next to them. Make sure they understand from which direction the cue will be taken – who speaks before whom and after whom – and let them practise speaking in turn. You may need to prompt most of the children by name the first time, gradually moving on to pointing or nodding at the ones who don't come in, until the whole group can manage to concentrate and participate in the activity without direct help.

In this way, children can feel and understand with their bodies and their voices how to wait for their turn to come and then confidently take the turn at the right moment, knowing that others will listen to them as they have listened. When they are much older and able to read, the children will be able to move on to taking cues and speaking lines from a script, provided they have practised turn taking in this way when they were younger.

When children are seated as a group, they can be encouraged to share and discuss dramatic ideas. Try some simple themes at first and increase the complexity as your children become more experienced and confident speakers. Make it clear that their ideas are interesting and important to you and to the others in the group and that they may choose to say anything they think is relevant.

SHARING MIMES

Mime the opening of an exciting birthday present in a big box and ask children in turn to tell you what is inside. Some will choose toys or sweets, while those who have developed greater skills in imagination might think up something unusual, such as 'a baby tiger' or 'a pink monkey', or something that wouldn't really fit into a box, such as 'a blue whale' or 'a combine harvester', and enjoy making you and the other children laugh or be surprised.

Mime walking through a jungle or forest and pretend to see a scary creature, then ask the children in turn which creature they saw. Some will think logically about the dramatic setting and name an animal that might be found in a jungle, such as a lion or a snake, or in a forest, such as a bear or a wolf, while some will think more dramatically and choose a fantasy creature, such as a dragon or a giant. Some will just focus on what might scare them and believe that it would be possible to find a crocodile in a forest or a goose in a jungle. There are no wrong answers! Remember that the purpose of this activity is actually to teach children to wait for their turn, listen to others and then speak out confidently to the group.

Work on a mime or action song activity involving running across a field of flowers, then ask the children in turn:

> How far did you run, Jonathan?

or   Did you sit down or roll in the flowers, Isabel?

or   Who ran with you, Lydia?

FIGURE 9.1 Ask each child to tell you which imaginary creature they are scared of

A few children nearing the end of the EYFS might try to describe the distance they ran or how long they were running in standard or non-standard units, such as 'twenty miles' or 'a hundred steps', 'ten minutes' or 'till lunchtime'. Younger ones are more likely to say that they ran 'round and round like a pony', or 'up to the clouds', or that they were running 'as long as an elephant could run', or 'until my legs couldn't work any more'. This is a correct response and dramatic and expressive similes should be very much encouraged.

It is very interesting to note which children always choose sensible, logical answers, such as 'racing like an athlete' or 'jogging all day long', and which children always choose something imaginative, such as 'bouncing like a kangaroo with big leaps' or 'running out to look for mouse food and hiding back under the flowers'. Some will vary from day to day, depending on their mood. This can offer you an insight into the children's personalities and can be helpful in speeding up the making of relationships with new children and the meeting of their individual needs if you only see them for an hour or two once a week.

As children grow older and more experienced, try asking them to imagine and discuss their ideas before acting them out, rather than afterwards. This requires more advanced thinking skills. Again, the focus of the activity is on waiting, listening and taking a turn appropriately, but the range of ideas can be celebrated too.

Ask each child in turn to tell everybody which jungle animal they will be. Then let them all act out the animals together at the same time. Or ask each child in turn to describe their favourite piece of play equipment in the park and then let them all act out the movements that they would use to play on the equipment. Children working at an advanced level may be able to take turns to make a suggested or chosen expression to the child next to them or to mime or act out an animal or an action in turn for the rest of the group to guess or copy.

If you have a selection of hats or masks for role play activities, you could invite children to take turns to try on a hat or mask and become the character who would wear it. They could then give a speech as that person or make noises as that animal, or they could perform some relevant actions or act out a part of a familiar story involving the character.

A child dressed in a police officer's helmet might decide to say: 'Now then, what's going on here? I'm arresting you! Move along there please!', or pretend to be directing traffic at a junction. A child wearing a pig mask might choose to make grunting sounds and roll in the mud or pretend to be building a house and hiding inside from the wolf.

■ **FIGURE 9.2** Dressing up in masks and hats helps children explore creatures and characters

Hats, masks, paws, shoes, tails and tabards for animals and 'people who help us' are the most readily available accessories to make or buy and the easiest characters to portray, but any role play outfits that will appeal to a particular group of children can be introduced.

LISTENING TO EACH OTHER

There are few more appreciated skills in the world than that of being a good listener. People who can be relied upon to really listen and take in what others are saying, offering real support and only appropriate help in difficult or confusing situations, are much sought after as counsellors and the type of strong friends that everybody wants to have.

Listening to others is also an important part of good manners and shows courtesy for the rights and feelings of those around you. Shouting out answers instead of putting up a hand or waiting to be asked, or offering an opinion without waiting for the speaker to finish or indicating your wish to comment, is behaviour that is frowned upon and not expected in normal circumstances. Appropriate behaviour skills must be learned in early childhood and practised until they may be used confidently in any situation.

Begin by teaching the children to listen to you. In most situations, there needs to be a leader who explains what is going to happen or what is required and asks whether everybody understands, whether they agree or whether they have any problems. Other adults must stop talking and listen to what the leader says once the session begins, to set the right example to the children, and they should also help and encourage all children to pay attention and stop distracting others. Young children may not yet know that listening to somebody when they have something valuable to say or when they have been placed in authority is the correct thing to do, but they can learn it very easily if they experience a consistent environment where adults and children respect each other. This is an important learning objective within the prime area of Personal, Social and Emotional Development (Making relationships).

When you ask a child a question, use the child's name and indicate by the tone of voice you use that this child has been chosen to speak and everybody else should listen for the next few moments. Promote good listening skills by ensuring that each child has a turn to speak and is not hurried or corrected. When children are not yet ready to speak alone, they may choose to take their turns by whispering to you or to another adult or child, or simply indicate that they do not wish to speak today. Do not try to force children to speak or make them feel inadequate because of their decision, but offer the same chance again, without fuss, at each session until they choose to participate. Then praise the child for the contribution, but not too much or you may undo the confidence that has been so newly gained.

Maintain eye contact with each child throughout the speech, proving that you are listening and taking a real interest in what is being said. Encourage the other children to look towards the speaker too (without staring too much) and to sit or stand still and quietly to avoid distracting others and missing vital words. Some children will look at the floor or their hands while they speak, until their confidence increases, but work towards them looking at the person they are speaking to and using body

FIGURE 9.3 Encourage children to listen to each other and wait their turn to speak

language to further facilitate communication. A child who shouts out or interrupts when another child is speaking should be gently reminded that 'We are all enjoying hearing what Ernie has to say at the moment, so could you please listen too? Then we will all hear what you have to tell us when it's your turn in a minute.'

Children who are very young, inexperienced or still learning other basic skills and concepts will not be able to wait and listen quietly for their turn and should not be expected to do it until they are mature enough. All children interrupt at times when they become excited by or absorbed in the topic being discussed, or cause a distraction because they lose concentration, and an explanation may be all that is needed. If a child is gradually learning to control more impulsive speech or behaviour, reminders over a few sessions will often be enough to prevent further problems. A child who has definite difficulties in listening to others and waiting quietly for a turn to speak, possibly due to a special need, may need the one-to-one support of an adult during the appropriate parts of a drama session in order to achieve the objective and not disrupt the session for the other children.

79

If a child confidently takes their turn but their speech is unclear and you are unable to understand what they say, you could sensitively ask a parent or carer, the child's key person or another adult if they understood. They may be more aware of the way the child forms certain words or sounds and be able to 'translate' for you, so you don't miss the good idea that the child offered. If nobody understood, you could ask the child to repeat the idea once and try again. If you are still unsure, it may be best to pretend that you did understand and praise the child's contribution as usual! You may suddenly work it out much later in the day and be well prepared for the next session.

DISCUSSION OF IDEAS

Accept and praise all ideas, even if a child only copies or is helped to speak by an adult, but offer extra encouragement to very imaginative children and hope that others may try to emulate them.

Children may gradually begin to understand more subtle differences in whether or not it is appropriate to speak out or interrupt occasionally and when a whole group discussion would be more valuable than everybody listening to one person at length. For example, if one child says that they have found a favourite toy in a present or had a popular food for dinner, it may be satisfying to that child to hear one or more of the group agreeing that 'That's my favourite too' or 'I like that for dinner as well' and it will not disrupt the taking of turns within the circle. If a child says that they like something and another mutters that they don't, this is not a problem unless they say it in an unpleasant way or try to imply that the first child is wrong to hold a different opinion. It is constructive for children to learn that different people like different things and that discussing likes and dislikes is interesting. This is an important early learning goal within the specific area of Understanding the World (People and communities).

Be prepared to flexibly initiate whole group discussions, including shows of hands or votes on who likes one thing more than another, whenever you feel that this would be appropriate, but ensure that individuals also have their chance to speak alone afterwards if they have been waiting for their turn. Children will only agree to wait patiently if they are secure in the knowledge that turns will be taken fairly and overseen by an adult who doesn't forget whose turn it is or notice who has waited without interrupting or fidgeting.

As in all areas of learning, take notice of how much progress each individual child is making, rather than their overall ability level, and avoid comparing them with each other. Children move through the early years with widely differing levels of ability. Our task is to ensure that all children have the opportunity to fulfil their potential.

Chapter 10

Co-operation and teamwork

Although adult performers may occasionally sing, act a play or a monologue or tell jokes alone, even they are supported by an orchestra, a backstage crew or a production team behind the cameras. They may also need a prompt, costume designer, make up artist or props team. Performers must make good relationships with their teams. This may mean getting to know a large number of people very quickly, working with them and then leaving to join a new team, knowing that some may work together on another project in the future, while others may never meet again.

Whatever a person's contribution and whether or not they are seen 'in the limelight', they must see their role as a crucial part of their team's work and strive always to be conscientious and reliable and to get on constructively with those around them. The earlier this attitude is embedded within a child's conscience and understanding, the more successful they may later be in careers and personal lives.

IN PRIVATE CLASSES

It is important to be aware of which children see each other outside classes and to allow them to be together when appropriate. This may give them the necessary confidence boost to enable them to achieve high levels of involvement and embrace new challenges. Many people prefer to take a friend along with them to a new activity throughout their lives! However, a confident pair or group of children may make each other too excited to concentrate, or may struggle with feelings of competition or rivalry. A less confident pair or group may increase each other's nervousness or be unable to work individually, always hesitating to express themselves and copying each other.

Encourage children to be sensitive to others but quietly confident about what they would like to happen. They should come to the circle or group and choose an appropriate place for themselves. If a child becomes upset because they wish to sit beside a friend but there is no space there, you could politely ask another child if they would mind swapping places or ask all the children to shuffle round a little to make the desired space appear. Work towards the children becoming confident enough to ask this for themselves. Praise the child who says: 'Please could you move up a little bit, Ella, so that I can sit next to Evan?' or 'Can I swap places with you, Olivia, so that I can be with Annie and you can be with Pollyjean?'

Thank the child who agrees and moves when they are asked or lets a child squeeze in beside them. Especially thank and praise the child who moves around or shuffles closer to another to solve a potential problem or who welcomes another child into the circle or group and offers a place for them to sit, without being asked. A steady stream of younger and newer children joining a class or group usually ensures that the older, more experienced ones can feel important in gradually managing more and more independently.

IN A NURSERY OR SCHOOL SETTING

If children attend a setting regularly, they will become familiar with each other much more quickly and begin to work together as a team more easily in all situations. Children may make progress more quickly in some group activities in these settings, but this may be offset by them moving on after a shorter period of time, while others may attend a private class for two years or more.

With the professional support of other qualified staff working with you during drama sessions, you may be able to gradually encourage and develop the abilities of all children to work together, to allow successful new pairings and groupings to emerge who can learn to co-operate under supervision. All adults must be consistent in their approach to participation, courtesy and standards of behaviour, following your lead during sessions and discussing any issues that arise or differences in opinion later when the children are not present. Remember to praise the adults too! They will enjoy being appreciated when they turn in enthusiastic and accomplished performances to encourage the children in their care.

Children in the early years will also seek warmer and closer relationships with those adults who sing, dance, play music and act out stories alongside them. Not all early years practitioners would eagerly choose to lead drama, but, with the right encouragement and example, everybody can enjoy working together. The following activities contribute particularly to learning objectives within the prime areas of Communication and Language (Listening and attention, Understanding, Speaking) and Personal, Social and Emotional Development (Self-confidence and self-awareness, Managing feelings and behaviour, Making relationships) and also the specific areas of Literacy (Reading) and Expressive Arts and Design (Being imaginative).

ACTING OUT STORIES

The best teamwork can often be observed when children and practitioners act out a story together. Tell a story as simply as possible, or lead and guide a discussion on the storyline of a very well-known tale, using a book with lots of pictures, a comic, magazine or poster, or some toys, models or objects to illustrate the important characters and events in the story. Then suggest that everybody re-creates it together.

■ **FIGURE 10.1** Acting out a simple story together develops children's imaginative and teamworking skills

If a child stands up or shuffles around because they cannot see the pictures or objects well during a story, reassure them that they will each see in turn, or suggest where they might move to at this point while you wait, but never allow it to happen without comment and without resolving the problem immediately. If one child begins to break up the group in this way, the others will then be unable to see or concentrate either and will also move and, within two minutes, the team and the activity will have dissolved.

If you stand up and launch into the first happening in the story with enthusiasm, everybody should feel inspired to follow you! Narrate the storyline appropriately as your actions and expressions unfold, encouraging everybody to copy what you are doing, but not to imitate you exactly.

Praise every attempt you see to describe the story through actions, expressions, words, sounds and mimes and every sensible or interesting addition to the plot or characters offered by a child or adult.

This activity can also be enjoyed by groups of adults and children using puppets to portray the speeches, actions and emotions of the characters in the stories. If each adult works on a different favourite story with a small group of four or five children, great fun can be shared as the stories are acted out for the other groups to watch. Some children find this more attractive and less overwhelming than acting and performing as themselves and prefer to experience creative and imaginative drama in this way.

SEQUENCES

Undertaken in mime or with the addition of speech or sounds, sequences are very short 'mini stories' that children act out, either all together or in small groups for others to watch. Encourage children to look carefully at each other's work and to offer praise spontaneously if they see something that they particularly like. Supporting each other through performing together for others and becoming an appreciative or constructively critical audience, enables everybody to take pride in being a member of a team.

CELEBRATING DIFFERENCES

Without encouraging a culture of one child feeling that they are better than another, or one feeling inadequate because somebody else's performance is said to be more accomplished, a mild attitude of 'healthy competition' actually promotes better teamwork. If you ask 'Who can make the crossest face?' or 'Who can push the heaviest wheelbarrow?'

FIGURE 10.2 Children understand how to work as a team through performing together with the support of caring adults

everybody will put forth their best effort, giving you the opportunity to praise a few children (and adults) at a time. It is almost guaranteed that they will also become excited, laugh and have fun. Simply ensure that there are enough activities offered to enable you to praise different people each time and that you have mentioned everybody's name at least once.

Through a harmless feeling of 'I was one of the best at pushing a wheelbarrow, but my friend Carys was better at making a cross face', or 'Rosie can jump higher, but Henry can hop for longer', children can come to understand and accept that we are all good at different things and that people like to be friends with us if we can express and celebrate our various achievements together. As children grow older, life does become more competitive and this can be a good thing, if it is not taken too far. Competing with others can challenge us to make our very best efforts and give us the reward of feeling that we have done well.

Children need to learn how to win or lose, how to accept success or defeat gracefully, how to avoid feeling devastated when they don't come out on top, or be pleased but modest when they do and how to join in with congratulating others on their successes. They need to know that team players should not gloat over others or feel angry with them and that the most important thing is to be a good sport and play fairly. Confident people who take pride in their achievements but take care of other people's feelings are the most popular members of any team. Drama projects can begin to teach these crucial skills effectively from a very young age.

MANAGING BEHAVIOUR

Make sure that any parents or carers who stay for sessions are aware of the difference between 'sibling tiffs' and real disagreements. Brothers and sisters, cousins, next-door neighbours and close friends attending a class together may be more competitive or have more of a tendency to argue with each other than others in the class. Discuss the children's relationships with parents or carers (out of the children's hearing) and agree on the most effective method of dealing with any rivalry that might occur. What matters most is that the influential adults in the children's lives are consistent in the areas of discipline and expectations of behaviour.

Parents and nannies who have only one child (or one child and a small baby) may have had no experience at all yet of normal life with two or more children growing up together and may incorrectly judge sibling behaviour as 'naughty' or 'disruptive'. Some well-timed explanations and careful exposure to other families in a relaxed situation may prove to be an ideal learning experience for them and prepare them for what may be to come in their lives!

Chapter 11

Ending on a high

Wherever your flights of fantasy and imagination have taken you during a drama class, you will need to bring everybody back together to end the session as a co-operative group again. You should aim to leave both children and adults feeling inspired and exhilarated, but tired and ready to be calm again.

CIRCLE TIME

Gather everybody together by enthusiastically announcing the last activities and putting yourself in the right place to begin. Depending on your group and on the previous activity, you may find that you need to call out and clap your hands, or you may achieve a more constructive response by whispering and beckoning to the children.

Action songs are usually the most successful way to end a session with this age group and a circle ensures that all children feel equally valued and secure in the knowledge that they have their own place to sit or stand. Always ending your sessions like this indicates to the children in a very concrete way that the session is almost over and they will soon be changing what they are doing. Young children rely on this type of clue to understand the pattern of their day and are helped a great deal by the beginning and end of certain activities always being presented in the same way.

Peer group classes in schools and early years settings may enjoy ring games and many parents also find them easy to relate to when attending a private class. These games are valuable for encouraging confidence and social skills, form part of our children's heritage and can be very enjoyable. However, since you are teaching drama, you could include some excerpts from 'real' stage shows in the West End. Many of the most popular and

FIGURE 11.1 Teach children how to end the performance of a musical number with a flourish!

well-known shows contain a wealth of material that can be shared with young children. If you ask everybody to sing along and copy some very simple actions that you make up to fit the song, you can really end on a high!

Try to include holding hands within the circle at a particular point within the music and ensure that it goes on long enough for all children to have found the hands of the people either side of them if they wish to, as this demonstrates the togetherness of your group as a drama company. Ensure that the excerpt you choose ends with a flourish and show children how to finish with their arms held high and a big smile.

Other simple movements and actions that you could use include:

- clapping hands (high and low, in front, to the sides and behind you);
- stamping feet (while standing or sitting);
- jumping or hopping;
- snapping fingers;
- clicking heels or knocking knees together;

89

- swaying bodies;
- swaying arms in the air;
- spinning around;
- tapping shoulders or knees or the floor;
- pointing to everybody in the circle with a moving finger;
- nodding or shaking heads;
- beckoning with a whole hand;
- 'sunshine' arms overhead;
- wiggling fingers;
- standing up and sitting down;
- parts of the hand jive!

You could also consider using a song that involves 'growing'. Children enjoy pretending to grow from a seed, in a crouched position on the floor, to a plant, flower or beanstalk, standing tall with arms outstretched or reaching as high as they can. This can make an excellent climax if used as an ending song. All opportunities to move, use and control the body contribute to the achievement of early learning goals within the prime area of Physical Development (Moving and handling).

KEEP SOME FUN RIGHT TO THE END

Save one or two songs that have become the children's favourites, as they may become tired and need that encouragement to stay with the group right to the end. Rather than watching people drift off one by one and allowing the session to peter out in an anticlimactic way, you want everybody to come running to join in with the last activity because it is so much fun! Particular movements may be popular with a group of children, such as flying like birds or aeroplanes or crawling like mini-beasts and it may be appropriate to find songs that involve those to encourage them all to join in. Young children especially love to attempt the movement made by some caterpillars that involves pulling up the back half of the body and then stretching the front half of the body forward and back down to the floor. This must be demonstrated by the class leader and necessitates crawling and rolling on the floor, but can cause much hilarity and is great fun. However, I have discovered that, although children can keep the movement up for a while, adult muscles will definitely ache the next day if it is tried for too long! Colleagues, parents and carers will appreciate it if you warn them of this and suggest that they watch the caterpillars more often than joining in with them.

FIGURE 11.2 Children love making movements like caterpillars and other mini-beasts

Not every session will be totally successful for all children right to the end, but it is important to retain your enthusiasm for the song, the actions and the group until you have finished in the way you intended. Those who have stayed with you will appreciate your stamina despite the distractions around. And, on another occasion, it will be different children who manage everything. More and more often, as their dramatic experience grows, it will be everybody.

VALUE RELATIONSHIPS

You should aim to build constructive relationships with each child, carer and key person. Value these relationships and the pleasure that they can give to you and to those you are working with. Drama is an activity that can encourage friendships, which might otherwise never have occurred. If possible, allow for some relaxed time immediately after a class during which the adults may chat and exchange ideas and any concerns. Sometimes a parent or key person will find it easier to talk with you after the drama session has 'warmed up' their confidence and your relationship.

Always thank children and adults, whether colleagues or clients, at the end of a session and congratulate them for working hard. Tell them that you have enjoyed working with them and look forward to seeing them next time. Accept thanks from adults gracefully and don't confuse children by refusing to allow them to hug you when they say goodbye if their wish to do so is spontaneous and not in any way initiated by you. Children in the early years like to express themselves with their whole bodies – and so do stage people! For many people, this type of closeness is a natural extension of drama and stagework and so it may be particularly appropriate at this time, when engaged in naturally and openly.

MOVING ON

Children continue to grow older and move on to new experiences throughout their lives. At the end of each school term and year, you will find that some or all of the children in your classes will have to leave you, which can, of course, feel sad. It is important to express your feelings in a controlled and appropriate way and to allow the children to express theirs. Lead by example, saying how you will miss seeing them each week and that you will always remember how good they were at some of the dramatic activities. Allow them to express how they feel in any way they feel able to do so. Some may talk about their feelings, some may draw a picture or make a card for you, some may be upset, while others may suddenly exhibit challenging or 'out of character' behaviour because they feel unable to cope with the impending changes in their lives.

Try to leave children with a firm understanding that they will have their memories and skills forever and will be able to use them in greater projects as their lives continue. It is fun to look back, but important to look forward and embrace new challenges with the strength gained from earlier ones. If you see any of the children in the future, greet them with pleasure, as old friends.

Whether or not you hold regular performances with your groups or classes, it is appropriate for young children to create a display or a show towards the end of a school year. Parents, families and friends enjoy an opportunity to see what their children have been learning and they will wish to mark the 'leaving' and 'moving on' with a memorable event. This will also help the children to feel that their time and work with you achieved a satisfactory climax. And then – what a good excuse for a party!

Chapter 12

Performance skills

Most young children enjoy the opportunity to be the centre of attention and 'show off' when they feel secure within a situation and a group of people. Offering them regular opportunities to stand onstage and speak, act, mime, sing or dance allows them to discover, develop and display their natural expressive abilities and enjoy sharing them with an audience, achieving early learning goals in the prime area of Personal, Social and Emotional Development (Self-confidence and self-awareness).

USING A STAGE

If you are lucky enough to have a stage, introduce the concept carefully, as many children may be fascinated but some may be nervous of standing on a raised floor surface with others looking at them. Begin by climbing on to the stage and standing there yourself, while the children remain on the floor level. Ask them if they can see you and why they can now see you more easily than when you were all on the floor together. Explain that performers stand onstage to allow their audience to see them clearly. Invite them all to join you onstage and stand there together. Then step down yourself and exclaim from the floor how well you can now see the children.

Take all safety aspects into careful consideration and be extra vigilant in supervision. If there are steps up to the stage, make sure that all children can climb them easily. If any of the children are very small or have additional physical needs, assist them sensitively by offering them a hand or arm to grasp as they step up, so they may let go as soon as they feel safe and are not made to feel different. If a child is wary of the steps or standing onstage, allow them to walk up and stand beside you or another child who is happy to be sensitively helpful. If all of the children are small but daring, insist that they all accept a guiding hand when moving up on to or down from the stage, to avoid any tripping and falling accidents and do not allow them to leap off wildly!

Do not force a child who is genuinely worried or upset by the idea of standing onstage, but allow them to watch the others a few times and then gradually encourage small progressions, such as climbing up and then immediately stepping down again, then standing onstage with you or another child but just watching and listening, then speaking, singing or dancing within a group of friends, before attempting to do anything alone.

Explain to all children that they must never stand too close to the edge of a raised stage, as it is easy to accidentally step off and it may be a long way down. Always stand at the front of a stage, or ask any assisting adults to do so, to remind children when their feet are too close to the edge and to catch a child if they do take a step too far! If the floor surface before the stage is very hard, you could place a gymnastic mat, floor cushions or a soft rug there to break a fall, just in case. Look for markings on the stage or mark out a line with chalk or coloured sticky tape and impress upon children that they should always stay behind the line.

A DESIGNATED STAGE AREA

If you do not have access to a stage, mark out an area on the floor to use. Depending on the floor surface and whether you have to remove the markings after each session, use chalk, coloured sticky tape, gymnastic mats, rugs, blankets or a piece of carpet. Introduce the area to the children as a special place to be, always refer to it as 'the stage' and treat it in the same way as a raised stage, entering from the back or sides but not the front. However, you need not worry about the safety aspects in the same way, as children may access it easily from the floor and will not come to harm if they 'fall off'.

THE RIGHT WORDS

Young children absorb language rapidly and love new, long and special words. They do not consider one word to be more complicated or hard to remember than another, but respond constructively to any words that are introduced in a meaningful context and used regularly within activities and instructions they can understand. Never be afraid to use the correct words for activities and names for parts of the stage, items used in stagework and people who work in the theatre. Teach them through the playing of games and then include them naturally in conversation and when explaining what you would like the children to do.

Here are the most useful ones to help you, in case you were not stage trained yourself!

DIRECTIONS

Upstage	Away from the audience, towards the back of the stage.
Downstage	Close to the audience, towards the front of the stage.
Stage left	The side at your left hand when you are standing onstage, facing the audience.
Stage right	The side at your right hand when you are standing onstage, facing the audience.
Stage centre	In the middle of the stage.

These terms can be combined to give instructions or play movement games. For example:

Stand at downstage centre, then move upstage and face stage right.

The group at upstage left moves to downstage right, then the group at downstage left moves to upstage centre.

You will notice that the terms *stage left* and *stage right* are very important. A group of people within a cast who are asked to move merely to the right or left may interpret that to mean different things, which could be disastrous in a dance routine! The audience's left and right are opposite to the performers' left and right, unless the performers have their back to the audience. Of course, there are times within a dance or mime sequence when they may turn their backs, but usually they will be required to face front. Therefore, everybody needs to remember that *stage left* and *stage right* refer to performers' directions when standing onstage and facing the audience.

It is correct to say *onstage* and *offstage*, without the addition of the word 'the' in the middle. Children can be invited to *enter* and *exit*, as well as 'come on' and 'go off'.

NAMES AND PLACES

Wing	The area at the side of the stage where performers may wait and through which they enter and exit. These are described as the *stage left wing* and the *stage right wing*.
Green room	A room or extended wing area in which performers wait to go onstage. (It does not have to be painted green!)
Greys	The curtains at the back of the stage, which, in a real theatre, are grey or silvery in colour, to prevent unwanted shadows caused by reflected light.
Backrun	The passage behind the greys through which performers and backstage crew can walk to pass between one wing and the other, unseen by the audience.
Housetabs	The main curtains that cover the stage before and after a performance and can be pulled for scene changes.
Auditorium	The place where the audience sits to watch a performance.
Front of house	All the areas used by the audience and not by the performers – auditorium, refreshment and waiting rooms, etc.
House lights	The main lights within the auditorium and other public areas.
Stage lights	The spotlights that are trained on the performers and light up the stage.

House lights and stage lights do not come on together. The house lights are turned off by the front of house team before the stage lights are turned on, and are turned on again after the stage lights are off. The correct stage terms are lights up and lights down.

Backdrop	A relevant picture painted on or created from fabric and hung or pinned to the greys behind the actors as a display to set the scene.
Set	Pieces of free-standing scenery carried on and offstage when needed.
Props	Objects used onstage to add to the story or develop the characters. Short for 'properties'.
Costume	Clothes worn to create characters or effects onstage.
Script	Book or sheet of words and directions that everyone on and behind stage follows and adheres to. (Can also be called 'Libretto'.)
Score	Book or sheets containing music and song words for musicians and singers to follow.
Lyrics	Song words.
Lines	Words said onstage – can be learned from a script or improvised around an agreed idea or storyline.
Cue	The word or action that occurs immediately before a performer's part, indicating that it is now his or her turn.
Prompt	A reminder of a line or what to do next, given by someone following a script in a wing.
Act	Part of a show between the beginning or end and an interval – usually two in a performance, sometimes three.
Scene	A section of a show after which there is a change in characters, storyline or setting.
Musical number	A song and/or dance routine performed as an integral part of a show.

PEOPLE

Producer	In overall charge of a production, taking care of all the tasks that have to be completed, from hiring of venues and staff to organising of tickets and refreshments.
Director	Arranges rehearsal schedules, plans and leads rehearsals, helps those onstage to perform to the best of their abilities and liases with backstage crews and lighting technicians to ensure the smooth running of the show. In smaller and amateur companies, one person often takes on the role of Producer and Director, but it is a huge amount of work and responsibility.
Choreog-rapher	Plans, sets, demonstrates and teaches dances and movement sequences.
Musical director	Arranges, teaches and plays or conducts music for songs and instrumental sequences.
Cast	Everybody who performs onstage during the course of a production.
Technician	In charge of setting up technical equipment and making it work appropriately throughout performances. Lighting technicians and sound technicians may work separately, or one person or team may arrange both.
Stage manager	In charge of sets, props, housetabs and any special effects throughout performances. Co-ordinates and directs the backstage crew.
Backstage crew	Responsible for moving and changing sets, supplying and removing props, opening and closing housetabs and operating special effects, under the direction of the Stage manager.
Front of House team	Responsible for the safety of the audience. In charge of checking tickets, keeping a headcount tally, showing patrons to their seats, selling programmes and refreshments, monitoring audience behaviour and evacuating the building in the event of fire.

ADAPT TO THE NEEDS OF YOUR GROUP

No child in the early years needs to learn all of these names, but many of them will enjoy learning a few and it is best to use whichever seem most appropriate to the work you are doing. You may use some in one term and different ones in the following term, returning to a few old ones and adding new ones the next year.

Since everything needs a name or a label to ensure that everybody knows what is being discussed, it makes sense to use correct ones from the beginning to avoid later confusions or having to learn everything twice.

SPEAKING ONSTAGE

Children can learn to chant in unison to give them the encouragement and confidence that they need to speak onstage. This can make a good introduction to a performance.

For example:

Hello everybody and welcome to our show! (or the name of your class or setting)

We are the little pigs!

Teddies love Christmas!

Monkeys live in the jungle!

Encourage the children to remember the skills they have acquired and practised in enunciation and voice projection and to speak loudly and clearly without shouting. Ask them to maintain a sensible speed and not to slow down while waiting for each other to come in. There is nothing worse for an audience than having to listen to a group of children groaning and grumbling along together at the rate of one word a minute! Praising a child who is a good leader for their confident speech and correct speed usually ensures that they will work hard to maintain it and encourage others to follow them. Impress upon the children that it is good to be the one who is heard by the audience to be confidently leading the others.

Wherever possible, allow children opportunities to speak individually onstage from the youngest age. They may take turns to hold a microphone, if they have already practised this during classes, so that they know when to speak and feel confident they will be listened to and heard by their fellow cast members and their audience. It can be helpful to families

FIGURE 12.1 Children speaking or chanting in unison can make a good introduction to a performance

forming an audience to have that small amplification, as well as an indication of exactly when their particular children will be speaking. Children who have positive experiences of speaking onstage during the early years are unlikely to develop any real shyness or self-consciousness about public speaking later in life (even if they feel that they must occasionally pretend to be embarrassed at certain stages and in certain situations, to fit in with their peer group).

If there are only a few children, saying their names, ages and ideas on a theme in turn can be enchanting for an audience of families and friends to watch and listen to. If they retain their natural spontaneity and say something amusing, be proud of their confidence and allow the audience to enjoy the joke in a sensitive manner. Very young children usually enjoy laughter around them and join in when they hear it. If you have a large group of children, you could arrange for them to speak in small groups, or, if you perform regularly, offer just the oldest children opportunities to speak individually, so that each child understands that they will have their turn when they are the oldest in the group.

If a child is suddenly reluctant to speak, even if they are usually the most talkative of all, just prompt them or speak for them and move on

FIGURE 12.2 Children enjoy using microphones to deliver their best speeches to their audiences

without fuss. There will always be some surprises in performance. The boldest child may be overwhelmed and the quietest may have been saving it all for the big occasion!

Children who are afraid to speak onstage or into a microphone at all at the age of 2 or 3, but who learn, practise and experience drama regularly, may soon be competing with each other in a friendly way to give the best speech. Within a year, children may take part in two or three successful performances and a couple of inaudible whispered names onstage may give way to such polished comedy routines as 'My name's Gabriel and I'm twenty-nine!' 'Well, my name's Phoebe and I'm forty-three and a half!'

A SIMPLE PERFORMANCE

The most successful children's performances usually rely on action songs, dances and mime sequences and acted stories set to music. If several children are singing, dancing or acting together, each part will be remembered by somebody and they will happily copy each other and work together to achieve the whole scene or musical number. It is also entertaining for an audience to watch the children playing a short game of Musical Statues onstage, because they love to freeze in interesting shapes and usually concentrate hard and then giggle!

Remind the children that the audience would like to see their faces, so they should try to remember always to face front when they are singing or speaking. Encourage them to smile all the time, unless they are making another expression during an acted sequence, and to sing as much of each song as they can.

Ensure that the children have had lots of opportunities to practise everything they will perform and that they feel confident of what to do. This means putting songs, sequences and speeches into an appropriate order and practising them in this order many times before the performance. Children will only be confident if they are sure of which song or activity comes next, what the music will sound like and where they will be standing or sitting at the beginning and end of each number.

IN A NURSERY OR SCHOOL SETTING

You will probably be asked to arrange for the children in your class or group to perform at least once a year, as part of a Christmas entertainment or an end of year celebration in the summer. There may also be other special events that your setting participates in.

Sometimes a class or group will provide their own performance separately; sometimes they will form a part of the whole entertainment in conjunction with the rest of the school or early years setting. If you are not totally responsible for the whole performance, make sure that you spend enough time talking with colleagues to plan and agree responsibilities and how each class or group will fit in. If you have any particular needs for your performance, such as set pieces or props or extra facilities to accommodate children with special needs, decide in advance how you will provide them with the minimum of fuss and practise this before the big day.

All staff members will be present for a performance in their setting and will have rehearsed with the children over the preceding weeks. You may decide that it is best for one or more of the adults to perform with the children or to be onstage with them to offer moral support and ensure safety. Or you may feel that the children are able to perform alone if adults sit behind or to the sides of the stage or in the wings or backrun to guide them on and offstage and to be close enough to help if needed. Each child should be able to see a familiar teacher or key person easily from the stage. Encouraging smiles are all that most of them will need to make sure that they give their best efforts and enjoy themselves in performing.

IN PRIVATE CLASSES

If you run weekly classes for children privately, it is not an absolute requirement that you arrange for them to take part in any performances. But, since drama is essentially a performing art, it is a rewarding thing to do and many parents may request or expect a number of opportunities to watch their children onstage. We all work harder and with more enthusiasm if we know that we are working towards an end product we can be proud of.

Try to arrange for a performance at least once a year. If possible, arrange for one at the end of each term because many clients may not stay with the class for a whole year, so some children could miss out on this valuable opportunity. Children in the EYFS mature, develop and change so quickly that they can make enormous progress within ten to twelve weeks and there is no easier or pleasanter way of displaying this to parents than to invite them to watch their children perform.

You may choose to perform onstage with the children and this can be a valuable opportunity to display your own skills to the children's families and to let them see the good relationship you have with each child. However, you must be sure of your own ability to concentrate and motivate the children throughout the performance and enjoy the experience yourself. You may have to carry on despite a strong desire to laugh, as children are marvellously unpredictable and will always surprise us! (The hardest act I ever had to follow was when we were performing a mime about putting a horse into its stable and one of my most adorable 4 year olds suddenly announced clearly to the audience, 'My horse is going to have her baby now – would you like to watch?')

If the children are happy to perform without you, you could consider standing behind the audience to offer encouragement and reminders. But do ensure that you are not a distraction to the audience or irritating to the children! Never sit or stand in front of the stage to watch or demonstrate where you will obscure the audience's view and spoil their enjoyment of their children's performance. They would rather see the odd mistake than try to see past the backs of wildly grinning and gesticulating

103

teachers, who are bobbing up and down, desperately mouthing words and miming actions! (As a mother of four children, I know this, having sat in the audience and experienced this inappropriate type of 'help' during school productions!)

You will need to ask colleagues to operate sound equipment and house tabs for you. Make sure you discuss and rehearse the performance with them before the children arrive. If you are performing with the children, ensure that a colleague or a trusted parent or nanny is seated close to the stage area and ready to help a child to leave the stage if necessary. Children in the EYFS should not be expected to 'get it all right', but they should not be left onstage in performance if they are disrupting or upsetting the other children, or if they are unhappy or likely to try to climb down on their own. It is possible to quickly and sensitively remove children during a performance and return them to parents, carers or teachers without upsetting anybody else. You should discuss this eventuality with the children's families and carers in advance and ensure they understand that this is the way their children would be handled.

Depending on the clients in your groups or classes, you may decide that it would be best to make the last class of term a performance, followed by a party. Or you may decide to offer a separate performance session and make attendance optional. This will depend on whether you feel that extended family members would like to attend and would find it easier at a weekend, or whether it would be better for your group to keep the audience small and invite only the adults who usually attend the classes.

You may have a group of children whose ages and abilities are very mixed and some may be very ready to perform while others are not. In this case, you may need to keep the performance separate and advise parents and carers carefully on whether they should consider attending to participate, to watch, or wait until their child is older or more confident. Or you may have a peer group class of children who should all have the opportunity to participate and therefore you might need to stick to the day and time of their usual session, in case any families are not free to give up extra time at the weekend or whenever you choose.

If you do offer a separate performance session, you will need to consider whether you should arrange for refreshments on that day and how to arrange seating and limit audience numbers to adhere to required safety guidelines. You will also have to arrange for the extra hire of your venue and some colleagues to help on the day, so you may need to ask parents to contribute towards this through the payment of a small 'performance fee'.

You will need to impress upon parents that they must make a decision in advance about whether their children are ready and keen to take part, let you know their decision and then stick to it. Tactfully offer advice, but ensure that it is each child's main carer who makes the final decision (not the children, who are not ready to understand at that level). They know their own children best and the occasion is only likely to be a success if they are fully supportive.

It is, of course, impossible to gain absolute reliability from such young children and their busy families. You may still find that one or two children fail to turn up after all, because they are unwell or their car breaks down, but the majority of your group should be secure. Avoid relying on any one child to say a particular line or lead a particular song or movement, but rather rehearse two or three in each role, or one or two from each class if several are coming together, to perform together or cover for each other. If a child suddenly refuses to go onstage on the day, just allow them to watch with their family in the audience.

If your performance is separate, you will need to make the last session of the term special for the children in another way. If you hold your performance during the weekend just before the week of your last classes, you can invite all class members to participate in the 'after-show and end-of-term party' at their usual session time during the last week of the term.

Providing background music and a themed craft activity for children to access on arrival creates a party atmosphere, different from other sessions, and encourages adults and children to work and chat together from the beginning. Make it very clear to parents, carers and children that everybody is welcome at the party, whether they performed or not, and allow them all to share in arts and crafts, dressing up in costumes, playing instruments, party games and refreshments in a relaxed and happy atmosphere.

COSTUMES

A group of small children dressed similarly in attractive outfits makes a performance look special and most young children love to dress up in costumes. It is always worthwhile to design and use costumes for a performance, but they do need to be simple to obtain and assemble and comfortable enough to wear.

Plain clothes, appropriate to the season, in colours that symbolise the animal or character being acted are an excellent base and can usually be supplied by the children themselves.

For example:

- white jumpers and tights for rabbits in winter;
- pink or black T-shirts and shorts for pigs in summer;
- blue sweatshirts, red trousers and wellington boots for winter soldiers;
- frilly dresses with wings and hairbands for summer fairies;
- long T-shirts tied with a sash or belt over shorts and 'dwarf' hats made from card or fabric for summer pixies or elves.

In summer, the children can perform in bare feet if the floor surface of your stage area is safe from splinters and other hazards, or ask them to wear plimsolls, ballet shoes, canvas shoes or sandals in keeping with their costume. In winter, they can wear an appropriate type of shoe or boot, or just socks or tights if the floor surface is safe and not slippery. If you are uncertain of the safety of your surface, use a non-slip mat or carpet for them to stand on.

Ears or headdresses attached to headbands of paper or card, or plastic hairbands can add the finishing touches to costumes. Make tails from card or fabric and attach them to the back of the children's costumes with a safety pin. This is quite safe, so long as all children are carefully supervised while wearing the tails and they are removed by adults as soon as the performance is over.

If at all possible, involve the children in making hats, ears and head-dresses and any other costume items or props that they would like for themselves during the days or weeks leading up to a performance, offering as much help and support as necessary. An adult could reinforce them or adapt them if necessary to make them strong enough for use, without altering the original ideas and designs, when the children are not present. They will then feel proud of their costumes and a greater ownership of their characters.

Allow them to take all of their costume pieces and props home after the show, or keep them to play with in their nursery or classroom. Much valuable role play can be developed when children's imaginations have been ignited by a real performance and they are immediately encouraged to continue to act, move, mime, dance and sing, using items and ideas in any ways they choose. This will enable them to achieve early

FIGURE 12.3 Encourage children to make their own costume items and props

learning goals in the specific area of Expressive Arts and Design (Being imaginative).

Thoroughly test any new costume ideas before going ahead with them in a performance situation! Children can become very upset and unable to perform if they are worried that their headdress will fall off if they move, or if they are asked to wear a mask without opportunities to practise wearing it in advance. Allow children to wear costume items in rehearsal or during free play periods to get used to them. It is important not to send all costume items home with children in advance unless you are sure they will all remember to bring them back on the day, but it may help one or two reluctant children to participate if they have been able to take them and practise wearing them with their familiar carers.

You may encounter some families who feel that their child cannot perform just because they are unable to provide the necessary costume items. You will need to explain to them that the decision should be based on their child's needs, not whether they can afford to buy a pink T-shirt or a pair of plimsolls and make it clear that you will arrange to lend costume items to any child who doesn't have them.

If you have children of your own, you might have spare or outgrown clothes in appropriate colours. If not, you may have friends and colleagues who do, or you could ask other parents to lend any spares that they have. Discuss individual children's and families' needs and preferences in a relaxed way well in advance and offer help as required. And always have spares of everything with you at the performance venue!

REMEMBER THE BOWS

Give enough time to teaching children how to take a bow. Begin with simple bows from the waist and move on to more elaborate ideas. Suggest that children have fun exploring new and different ways of taking bows. They may put their arms across their bodies or behind their backs, or sweep an arm before them with a twirling hand. They may hold hands in a line or stand separately in their own spaces. Explain to the children that taking a bow means 'I've finished. Thank you for watching.'

Teach children to accept and enjoy applause. They should be proud of their achievements onstage and understand that it is good to hear that an audience has appreciated your efforts enough to feel that they would like to clap.

REWARDS FOR EVERYBODY

Certificates and stickers are increasingly popular as rewards for this age group and they are fairly cheap and easy to buy or make in any quantity. It is often much appreciated by parents and children if you are able to provide these at the end of a performance or an end of term party. Whether you do this or not, make sure that you give the children lots of praise for their efforts and remember to thank them and their families for their support and commitment throughout the rehearsal and performance period.

A warm thank you and an offer of friendship within a professional relationship costs nothing, but gains a great deal – including the goodwill of clients who will stay for the following term and the next show and go on to recommend you, your classes or your setting to all their friends.

When parents and grandparents tell you how much they enjoyed a performance, or how their child talks excitedly all week about the drama class, or how the child's play has become more imaginative, more focused and more fun since they began attending classes, you know that you are succeeding in your aims. When children happily dance up to you whenever

■ **FIGURE 12.4** Taking a bow means 'I've finished. Thank you for watching'

they see you and immediately initiate a conversation, you know that you have helped them to build the confidence and self-esteem that will benefit them throughout their lives.

I am always most rewarded when children tell me how much they 'love drama and doing shows and talking to the class and pretending things with you.' As we leave the stage at the end of a performance, I feel that all of the hard work has been worthwhile if a child exclaims spontaneously 'And it was fun!'

If we can make drama accessible to everybody and give them the skills, the confidence, the social abilities and the enthusiasm to use it, we will contribute to making the world a better place for our children to grow up in – and how much more fun we will all have!

Appendix 1

Example plan for a simple drama session
(Approximately forty-five minutes)

Some examples of songs and music that could be used are given in italics, but practitioners may always select their own to suit their groups of children.

Introduction

Welcome everybody and sit in a circle to chat until all have arrived and are settled.

Opening action song

How Do You Feel Today? / Warm Up Time / Put A Smile On

Lead and demonstrate singing and actions with enthusiasm and encourage everybody to join in.

Move around the circle, offering to shake hands with each person in turn and saying clearly, 'Hello, my name is (Debbie).' Encourage children (and adults) to respond in a similar manner, taking your hand and speaking the sentence or just their name in return.

Expressions

Sit in two lines facing each other. Discuss how to use faces and bodies to show everybody how you feel – without any talking (called mime).

Demonstrate and encourage all children to join in with each expression:

happy; sad; cross; surprised; worried; tired; thinking; excited

Movement

Stand in spaces all over the floor. Discuss and practise moving in a variety of ways, explaining that music can help us all to move together with appropriate speed and rhythm.

Movement music or song

Let's Go Walking / Clap Your Hands, Touch Your Toes / The Wheels On The Bus

Demonstrate each movement as the music is played and encourage everybody to join in, moving around the space at random.

Speech, enunciation and cue taking

Sit in a circle again. Introduce a well known nursery rhyme or song and ask how many children already know it.

Nursery rhyme or simple children's song

Baa Baa Black Sheep / Humpty Dumpty / Miss Polly Had A Dolly / Twinkle Twinkle Little Star

Play the song for everybody to listen to. Then explain and demonstrate how to speak each word clearly (enunciation) and how to speak together as a group (in unison). Chant the nursery rhyme or song in unison with all children joining in and trying to enunciate.

Possible extension activity

Ask whether the children can fill in the missing word or sound when the speaker stops (taking a cue). Ask them to listen while you say the rhyme and stop suddenly at obvious places. Encourage the children to fill in missing words and sounds on cue.

Acting

Sit or stand in spaces all over the floor again.

Nursery rhyme or simple children's song (again)

Baa Baa Black Sheep / Humpty Dumpty / Miss Polly Had A Dolly / Twinkle Twinkle Little Star

Lead all the children in fitting actions to it, singing along as much as possible.

Character acting

Sit in a group to introduce the popular character(s) of the day. Inside your 'special bag', there will be appropriate soft toys and a poster, picture or book.

Tell a simple story about the character(s), encouraging the children to participate in the telling, and discuss how the character moves, walks or drives.

Move into spaces all over the floor again.

Character's theme song or music

Thomas the Tank Engine / Andy Pandy / Bob the Builder / Spot

Lead all children in acting out the story they have just heard, while the music plays, using as many different expressions and movements as possible.

Sit down at the end of a song or music to discuss what else the character always does or might do.

Character action song

Train Is A Coming / Here We Go Looby Loo / Building Up My House / The Quick Brown Fox Jumps Over The Lazy Dog

Stand up again in spaces. Lead and encourage all children to join in with an action or movement song that has a link with the character(s).

Listening skills

Sit in spaces all over the floor. Discuss how to listen carefully to music and stop when the music stops. Check that all children understand how

113

to dance and then sit down quickly, as in the party game Musical Bumps. Explain that the music will be suitable for lively, exciting dancing and that children may make up their own moves in whatever style they wish.

Dance music or popular song

Mamma Mia, Dancing Queen, Summer Night City – Abba/It's A Miracle, New York City Rhythm – Barry Manilow/Dancing In The Moonlight – Thin Lizzy

Lead dancing and game, following the music, and encourage everybody to join in.

Confidence skills

Ask the children to form a Follow My Leader line behind you (with support from adults).

Marching music

On The Stage/Let's All Go Down The Strand/The Grand Old Duke Of York

March around the room and on to the stage with all the children, while the music plays.

Voice projection

Stand onstage in a line or a group. Demonstrate how to speak loudly and clearly onstage. Suggest a few simple speeches. Allow the children to speak in unison.

Performance skills

Demonstrate to the children how to take a bow and allow them all to practise, together and then separately.

Marching music (again)

On The Stage/Let's All Go Down The Strand/The Grand Old Duke Of York

March back down to floor. Stand in circle again to finish class together.

Closing action song

Build It Up, We're Gonna Find A Way, One Brick At A Time — Barnum

Lead the singing and actions and encourage everybody to join in.

Thank everybody for coming and hope to see them all again next time!

Example plan for a more advanced drama session

(Approximately one hour)

Some examples of songs and music that could be used are given in brackets, but practitioners may always select their own to suit their groups of children.

Introduction

Welcome everybody and sit in a circle.

Opening action songs

It's A Wonderful Day Today! / *Hallo Everybody* / *Mister Sun* / *Clap Your Hands Just Like Me* / *My Little Red Fire Truck* / *One Potato, Two Potato*

Lead singing and actions with enthusiasm and encourage all the children to join in.

Shake hands with all the children around the circle and say clearly,

'Hello, my name is (Debbie).'

Encourage the children to look at your face, take your hand and respond with their names in a similar manner.

Expressions

Sit in two lines facing each other. Discuss how to use faces and bodies to show everybody how you feel — without any talking (called miming).

Demonstrate and encourage all children to join in with each expression:

happy; excited; sad; cross; thinking; having an idea; pleased; saying yes; saying no; saying please; asking somebody to come here.

Explain that one mime after another to create a very short story is a sequence.

Mime sequence

Demonstrate and encourage all children to think about and join in with each action.

feeling very tired, going upstairs, changing into pyjamas, cleaning teeth; looking for teddy, climbing into bed, falling asleep.

Movement

Stand in spaces all over the floor. Discuss how to move in different ways and how music can help us all to move together and with appropriate speed and rhythm.

Movement music or songs

Jump / I Went To School One Morning And I Walked Like This / You Can Stamp Your Feet / She'll be Coming Round the Mountain / Head, Shoulders, Knees And Toes / Wind The Bobbin Up

Demonstrate and encourage all children to join in with each movement as music is played and also to sing along to songs, moving around the space at random.

Speech, enunciation and cue taking

Sit in circle. Introduce a well known nursery rhyme or song and ask how many children already know it. Say it to them, deliberately getting key words wrong! Once they have all laughed at you and most of them have supplied the correct words, play the nursery rhyme or song for everybody to listen to.

Nursery rhyme or simple children's song

Hickory Dickory Dock / Little Miss Muffet / Tommy Thumb / I Can Play On The Big Bass Drum

Chant the nursery rhyme or song in unison with all children joining in and trying to enunciate as much as possible. Then repeat, missing out words and phrases, and ask the children to take their cues and fill in missing words, sounds and phrases.

Repeat again, asking each child to take a cue around the circle and supply the next line(s) – giving help and encouragement as necessary. The rhyme or song can be repeated as many times as necessary to include all children.

Acting and singing

Sit or stand in spaces all over the floor.

Nursery rhyme or simple children's song (again)

Hickory Dickory Dock / Little Miss Muffet / Tommy Thumb / I Can Play On The Big Bass Drum

Lead all children in fitting actions to it, singing along as much as possible.

Character acting

Sit in a group to introduce the popular character of the day. Hold up your 'special bag' and give clues to who is inside, encouraging all children to guess. Bring out the soft toy(s) and a storybook when somebody guesses correctly and allow children to speak to the toy(s) and handle them in turn if they wish.

Tell a simple story about the character using the pictures in the book, encouraging the children to participate in the telling and discuss the story.

Character's theme song or music

Pingu / Fireman Sam / Maisy Mouse / Barney the Dinosaur

Lead all children in acting out the story they have just heard – incorporating as many expressions, feelings, movements, mimes, words and actions as possible! (Maintain 'conversations' with the toy(s) throughout, as encouragement, rewards and links.)

Character action song

The Penguin Wears His Dinner Suit / Hurry, Hurry, Drive The Firetruck / A Mouse Lived In A Windmill – Ronnie Hilton / Walk The Dinosaur – Was (Not Was)

Lead and encourage all children to join in with actions and movements that have a link with the character.

Ask toys to congratulate the children and say goodbye and put them away in a bag.

Listening skills

Stand in spaces all over the floor. Check that all children understand how to dance while the music plays and stand very still as soon as the music stops, as in the game Musical Statues.

Dance music or popular song

High School Musical, All In This Together – High School Musical 3 / Hey Mr Music Man, Don't Stay Away Too Long – Peters And Lee / Don't Stop Me Now – Queen / Blame It On The Boogie – The Jackson 5)

Lead dancing and game, following the music, and encourage all children to join in.

Confidence skills

Ask the children to form a Follow My Leader line behind you.

Marching music

March around the hall and on to the stage with all the children while the music plays.

Voice projection

Stand onstage in a line or a group. Suggest a few simple speeches and allow the children to speak in unison. Then ask them each to speak individually, in turn, to say their name and age and a favourite colour, food, weather, etc. (linked to the story or character if possible).

Dance

Explain and demonstrate some simple repeating dance steps and movements.

Musical number

Sweet Gingerbread Man / Raindrops Keep Falling On My Head / Join The Circus — Barnum / Never Smile At A Crocodile

Children stand in spaces onstage. Perform a very simple set dance routine to an extract from a popular musical number, standing on the floor facing the stage and asking all children to try to copy you. Then ask each child in turn to take a bow.

Marching music (again)

Reach — S Club 7 / Summer Holiday — Cliff Richard / United We Stand — Brotherhood Of Man

March back to the floor as music plays again, to stand in a group and take a bow together.

Developing memory skills

Explain that you are going to learn a set of songs and dances gradually and that you will be able to perform to everybody in your show at the end of term, dressed as the appropriate characters! Tell them what the characters or animals will be.

Character or animal songs

Autumn term – for winter or Christmas performance

Goldilocks And The Three Bears / Where Oh Where's My Teddy Bear? / The Bear Went Over The Mountain / Teddy Bear, Teddy Bear

Dress as teddies

or

Galloping Through The Snow / I'm A Jolly Jolly Snowman / Jingle Bells / We Wish You A Merry Christmas

Dress as snowmen

Spring term – for Spring or Easter performance

Oats And Beans And Barley Grow / Old Macdonald Had A Farm / Dingle Dangle Scarecrow / To Market, To Market

Dress as farmers

or

Chick Chick Chicken / Good Morning Mrs Hen / Two Little Dicky Birds / Hot Cross Buns

Dress as birds

Summer term – for end of school year performance

The Beehive / Incy Wincy Spider / The Ants Go Marching / Caterpillars Only Crawl

Dress as mini-beasts

or

Walking Through The Jungle / Monkey Climbing In The Tree / Animal Fair / Three Little Monkeys Jumping On The Bed

Dress as monkeys

Lead and encourage children to copy singing, actions, mimes and movements, adding more refinements each week. Aim to include three or four songs of different types and introduce them one or two at a time, working up to practising all of them in one session by about half way through the rehearsal period.

121

Sit in a circle again to finish the session together.

Closing action songs

Stand Up Sit Down, Getting To Know You – *The King And I* / *Wiggly Woo* / *My Home Is A Castle To Me* / *Slap And Clap* / *Mr Coconut Man*

Lead singing and actions and encourage everybody to join in.

Thank everybody for coming and hope to see them all again next time!

All of the suggested songs and music listed within the example session plans as titles only can be found on the following CDs:

Rod, Jane And Freddy Onstage

Riggidy Jig and *Riggidy Jig 2*

Bang On A Drum (*Playschool* collection)

Singing Kettle (Scottish collections – various titles)

My Little Red Fire Truck (Canadian collection – four titles)

Barney The Dinosaur (various titles)

Tumble Tots (various titles)

Jo Jingles (various titles)

Round And Round The Garden, Food Glorious Food, Going To The Zoo,
Nellie The Elephant, Sing A Rainbow, The A-Z Of Children's Songs
and other titles from the *Early Learning Centre*

Collections of children's character theme songs and tunes
Collections of songs sung by popular children's television characters
Collections of nursery rhymes and popular children's songs

Other good songs and music to use may be found within well known musicals, such as:

Alphabet Zoo – Ralph McTell

Barnum, Cats, Starlight Express, Oklahoma

The Sound Of Music, The King And I, The Wizard Of Oz

SONGS THAT YOU COULD USE

Many suggestions for suitable nursery rhymes and popular children's songs are included within the example drama session plans.

Others that you could use (from the same CDs and other sources) are:

Nursery rhymes: *Rock A Bye Baby, Round And Round The Garden, Jack And Jill, Little Bo Peep, Ride A Cock Horse, Polly Put The Kettle On, Little Boy Blue, Hey Diddle Diddle, Three Blind Mice, Pop Goes The Weasel, London Bridge, Pat A Cake Pat A Cake.*

Children's songs: *I'm A Little Teapot, The Wheels On The Bus, Row Row Row Your Boat, A Little Rabbit On A Hill, Wind The Bobbin Up, I Hear Thunder, Little Cottage In A Wood, Sing A Rainbow, I'm Going To Build A Little House, Sleeping Bunnies.*

Counting songs: *Five Little Ducks Went Swimming One Day, Three Little Men In A Flying Saucer, Five Little Speckled Frogs, Ten Green Bottles, Five Brown Teddies, Six Little Ducks, Five Fat Peas, Ten Fat Sausages, Five Currant Buns, Ten Little Fingers, One Two Three Four Five Once I Caught A Fish Alive.*

Action songs: *If You're Happy And You Know It, Open Shut Them, Roly Poly, The Apple Tree, Tall Shop In The Town, Two Fat Gentlemen, The Cherry Tree, Jelly On A Plate, Jack In A Box, The Green Grass Grew All Around.*

Movement songs: *Little Green Frogs, Eight Rowers In A Boat, You Gotta Sing, An Elephant Walks Like This And That, This Is How I Ride My Pony, Henry The Crab, Look Both Ways, I'm A Fluffy Little Cloud, The Yellow Elephant, Chug Chug, This Little Bird, Going To Boston, Yellow Bird, The Big Ship Sails On The Alley Alley O.*

Ring games: *Ring A Ring O Roses, Did You Ever See A Lassie? There Was A Princess Long Ago, The Hokey Cokey.*

Practical and legal requirements

WORKING PERIPATETICALLY IN EARLY YEARS SETTINGS AND SCHOOLS

- Adhere to the lengths of sessions and the times agreed and allow time outside sessions to communicate with children's key persons and other colleagues.
- Ask for a written list of the first names of the children in each group and learn them by heart as quickly as possible, to ensure the control and safety of all children.
- Ask for a written list of the children's dates of birth or ages in years and months, in order to have age appropriate expectations and assess progress accurately.

TEACHING PRIVATE CLASSES

- Hire your own venue and check it for safety, cleanliness and suitability for use before allowing your clients to enter the premises.
- Ensure an adequate space with a safe floor surface and access to toilets appropriate for children's use.
- Provide a jug and suitable drinking cups and ensure access to clean drinking water within the premises. You could ask clients to bring their own drinks or water bottles, but some might forget. You might also need clean water for first aid purposes. Encourage children to drink before and after sessions and consider allowing a few breaks for drinks in hot weather. Keep drinks away from the main drama and movement area and wipe up any spills immediately, as a wet floor is a safety hazard.

- If possible hire a smaller venue, which allows you to hold your own key and be the sole user during your sessions, rather than a shared or community facility with an open front door and more than one group using the building and toilets at the same time.
- Clean and check the premises thoroughly before you leave and ensure that all necessary safety checks have been carried out after the last client has left and all doors locked securely. Report any problems with a venue immediately to the person in charge of hall maintenance.
- Arrive in time to prepare your venue and equipment and to turn on heaters or fans to ensure a comfortable temperature before clients come in.
- Allow extra time before and after sessions to chat with clients and answer queries.
- Provide a selection of children's books as a focal point for clients who arrive in good time and need to wait for others before the session begins.
- Keep an attendance register and mark each child present as they arrive. Also mark the number of adults and younger siblings attending.
- Update the register if any person arrives later or leaves earlier in case there should be a fire in the building and you need to evacuate. This is the law, because lives could be put at risk if an accurate head count cannot be established in an emergency.

CARRYING YOUR OWN EQUIPMENT

- Maintain your own equipment and make it easily transportable, as you must set it up and remove it again quickly at each session.
- Prepare as much as possible at home, leaving only furniture to move and bags to be opened on arrival.
- Pack things methodically back into their appropriate bags and take them home after the children leave, then keep them stored and ready for the next session. You will need:
  - a CD or other music player and the music that you intend to use (with copies or back-ups in case of accidents);
  - a bag of any other props that you intend to bring out later in the session;
  - your lesson plans on a clipboard;

125

- an attendance register;
- payment records and a lockable cash box containing change;
- information sheets with registration forms and any clients' letters;
- a first aid kit suitable for children;
- tissues and wet wipes;
- pens and paper;
- a mobile telephone.

TAKING PHOTOGRAPHS

- Ask for the permission of parents, guardians and carers before taking any photographs of children in performance or engaged in drama activities.
- Verbal permission is usually enough if the photographs will stay in albums in your possession and only be shown to class members.
- Written permission is needed for any photographs to be used in a book, publicity brochure or leaflet that may be sold or distributed to the public. You will need to provide a form that parents can sign to give this permission, detailing the purposes of the pictures and their likely distribution.
- Children's names should never appear with their photographs without a good reason and only with the express written permission of each child's parents or guardians.

MANAGING TIME

- Start and finish on time, as long as enough clients are present to make the experience valuable for the children, as clients are entitled to the full session that they pay for but some will have other commitments immediately after the classes.
- Let clients know that, if they are sometimes late, they are still able to join in at whichever point you have reached and the children will always be made to feel welcome.

INVOLVING OTHER ADULTS

- Ensure that you always meet the correct adult to child ratios, according to the children's ages. One teacher or early years practitioner may work with up to four 2 year olds or up to eight 3 year olds. In a school nursery or reception class, the ratio may be one adult to thirteen children. At least two adults must always be present with a group of children.

- Share lesson plans in advance and work constructively with colleagues in settings.
- Offer parents and carers the choice of joining in, watching, waiting in another room or leaving and returning at the end of the session.
- Ensure that you have correct contact telephone numbers to use if a child should be hurt, unwell or distressed or if an adult is delayed and does not return by the end of a session to collect their child.
- Read through registration forms regularly and memorise and use parents' and carers' names.
- Ask accompanying grandparents what their children call them; 'Granny', 'Grandma' and 'Nana' or 'Grandad' and 'Grandpa' sound like very different people to a child.

COSTS, BUDGETS, INVOICING AND ACCEPTING PAYMENT

- If you are employed within an establishment or by an authority to work in various settings, you will receive a salary and not need to deal with money.
- If you work on a private freelance basis, you must handle payments yourself.
- Settings have budgets and cannot always have exactly what they would like or what would be ideal for the children. But children can still benefit from a very short drama session each week, or a session once a fortnight or once a month. A large group of children could work together, if enough staff and space are available, or you could divide children into groups who take turns to participate in a session.
- Agree on a regular payment date with each setting and give them invoices in advance.
- Keep clear records of exactly how much is owed and how and when it should be paid.
- If you become involved with a setting that does not pay its bills, simply issue another invoice that states the date by which payment is due.

127

- If it seems unlikely that the setting can pay its bills, you will need to put in writing that you cannot offer any more sessions until the outstanding invoice has been paid.
- Set fees for private classes realistically.
- Research how much other groups and individuals charge for extracurricular activities for the same age range in your area, taking into account the staff they employ and the equipment and venues they use.
- Fees must not be too low to meet costs and provide you with a working wage, or you will quickly resent the amount of time and care that you put into your preparation and leading of classes and may seek to raise fees too soon or cut corners.
- Clients may consider that cheap classes will not be good enough, or enrol only because they are the cheapest option and not because they have any interest in their children learning drama.
- Keep fees at the same level for as long as possible, as most clients get used to paying particular sums regularly and only notice the increases.
- Offer a choice of payment options and keep a clear and visible record of payments that can be easily shared with parents, but ensure confidentiality.
- Allow clients to pay separately for their first class and then take home the necessary information and registration forms to return with further payment if they choose to continue, so that they will come to an informed decision and not take free trial classes without ever intending to make a regular commitment.
- Print out a standard slip of paper for outstanding fees, which you can fill in with a name and amount and hand out whenever a client forgets to pay. This keeps the money separate from the service and the people and avoids embarrassment on both sides.
- If you are unable to buy and use a portable machine to process card payments from clients, or to accept cheques, you may choose to give your clients the details of your separate drama teaching account, so that they can transfer payments directly, and you can also accept cash.

ADVERTISING AND COMMUNICATING VIA A WEBSITE

- Maximise your advertising to potential new clients by setting up an attractive, well designed and easy to use website. This can persuade new families to make contact with you and to come along to a class, where you can show them that it is as good as it sounds.
- Update the website regularly to display class times, term dates and fee details for existing clients, along with contact details and registration forms for new ones.
- Maintain paper copies of all details and registration forms to hand to clients personally when they attend a class, but also allow them to print out copies at home if they prefer to.

COMMUNICATING BY E-MAIL, TEXT AND TELEPHONE

- Make your e-mail address available to clients and request theirs on registration forms, so that you can easily communicate unavoidable changes to sessions, send reminders about fees, costumes or parties and offer holiday workshops or extra services.
- Do continue to communicate by telephone for last minute queries, changes or information and ensure that a parent or carer can be immediately contacted in that way if there is an emergency with a child during a session.
- Allow families to send text messages to say that they cannot attend a class, rather than not letting you know at all or leaving a message that you will not receive until later.

SAFETY TRAINING, CHECKS AND INSURANCE

- Before leading children's drama sessions, you must have completed the required training in first aid and child protection and have the certificates to prove it. Ideally, any colleagues assisting with the sessions will also have completed the training. You need a valid certificate in Paediatric First Aid or First Aid for Child Carers (gained from a twelve-hour course), which is renewed every three years, and a relevant Child Protection training certificate, gained through attending a course each year.

129

- Adults teaching or caring for children or vulnerable people, or having unsupervised access to them, must obtain a Disclosure and Barring Service (DBS) check from the Disclosure and Barring Service, which was established under the Protection of Freedoms Act of 2012, to merge the functions previously carried out by the Criminal Records Bureau (CRB) and the Independent Safeguarding Authority (ISA). Those working with children in the early years need an Enhanced DBS check (previously an Enhanced CRB check) to prove that they have no convictions, cautions, reprimands or final warnings and also that no relevant additional information about them is being held locally by police forces.

- The DBS also checks that adults are not barred from working in care and learning because they harmed or were likely to harm a child or an adult.

- A parent, carer or other family member or friend may watch or join in with a group of children participating in a class, but may not take any child other than their own out of the room separately for any reason, unless the child's parent or guardian has given express written permission. If a child prefers to receive help with personal needs from a familiar adult who is a family friend, you may allow it provided a staff member with the necessary checks and certificates is also present throughout.

- Explain these regulations very tactfully to trusted adults who are simply trying to be helpful and kind when a child needs extra attention and you are busy. Health and safety rules are very strict and can, at times, make things feel unnecessarily complicated or difficult, but they are there for our protection.

- If anybody other than staff, parents and carers enters the building or the room in which you are working with the children, you must ensure that you can see every child clearly throughout the time the person is on the premises and that they do not approach any child individually, or speak to the group.

- Take out appropriate insurance that covers public liability (and employer's liability if needed), as well as personal accident and injury to yourself and also to your private clients, staff and colleagues, if you have them.

- A registered setting or a venue that you pay to hire should already be insured.

- Whether or not you insure your portable equipment is a matter of choice.
- Be aware that your insurance will be invalid if you do not adhere to fire regulations and ensure the safety of your audience during performances. You must provide enough seats, with wide, clear aisles to each side of the auditorium and not exceed the registered seating capacity of the venue. There must be enough clearly marked, unlocked and unobstructed fire exits, with a member of the front of house team stationed beside each one and ready to direct the audience out of the building if necessary. Any wires or cables from lighting or sound equipment that run across the floors or walls must be fixed down and fully covered with appropriate tape.
- If you sell tickets for a performance, you must take out more complicated short term public liability insurance, but, if the tickets are free or only donations are asked for, you do not need to do this, as your usual level of insurance cover will be adequate. Most groups and settings would find it difficult to charge enough for their tickets to cover the insurance costs and will perform to a larger and more appreciative audience if they are only required to make a donation at the end or purchase programmes and refreshments.
- Use a reputable and well established specialist insurance company, such as Morten Michel, which offers tailor-made policies for those working in childcare and education, allowing you to choose exactly the right cover for your needs at a competitive price.

Index

Printed by PGSTL